The Perfect Present

My Best To You!

Robyn Spizman

other books by
ROBYN FREEDMAN SPIZMAN

The Perfect Present

THE ULTIMATE GIFT GUIDE
FOR EVERY OCCASION

ROBYN

FREEDMAN

SPIZMAN

CROWN PUBLISHERS, INC.
NEW YORK

This book is designed to provide general information in regard to the subject matter covered. At the time of initial publication, all of the information is believed to be accurate; however, some or all of the information is subject to change from time to time and may no longer be free of charge. No warranties or representations with respect to the information provided is made and neither the publishers nor the author shall be liable for any loss or damage to persons or property arising from the use of this book.

Published by Crown Publishers, Inc.,
201 East 50th Street, New York, New York 10022.
Member of the Crown Publishing Group.

Random House, Inc. New York, Toronto, London, Sydney, Auckland
www.randomhouse.com

CROWN and colophon are trademarks of Crown Publishers, Inc.

Printed in the United States of America

DESIGN BY KAREN MINSTER

Library of Congress Cataloging-in-Publication Data
Spizman, Robyn Freedman.
The perfect present : the ultimate gift guide for every occasion /
by Robyn Freedman Spizman.
1. Gifts.   I. Title.   GT3040.S69   1998   395—dc21   98–17544

ISBN 0-609-60131-8

10   9   8   7   6   5   4   3   2   1

First Edition

To perfect presents,
tried and true.
Dearest family and friends,
those gifts are you.

—RFS

Contents

Acknowledgments

*M*y appreciation goes to those individuals who continue to give precious gifts to me daily, especially my husband, Willy; our children, Justin and Ali; and my parents, Phyllis and Jack Freedman. Special thanks also go to Doug and Genie Freedman, Gus and Regina Spizman, Sam Spizman, Grandma Pauline Blonder, Aunt Francie Ritchkin, Lois and Jerry Blonder, Ramona and Ely Freedman, Bettye Storne, and my entire family for a lifetime of encouragement.

To my fabulous editor, Alexia Brue of Crown Publishers, for her wonderful assistance and inspiration; to Tina Constable, Kate Reid, Karen Minster, and Robin Strashun for their dedication and hard work on behalf of this book; to Sharon Squibb and Lara Webb for cheering me on; and to my outstanding literary agent, Meredith Bernstein, for her continued support and persistence on my behalf. My appreciation also goes to Sandy John for her dedication and relentless research on behalf of this project, and to Marla Shavin for her clever contributions.

Also to the following individuals who inspired me and shared their perfect presents: Ken Fritz, Kailie Rubin, Jack Morton, Jim Braude, Mary Billingsley, Eileen Silverman, Patty and Larry Brown,

Betty and Alan Sunshine, Marianne and Stephen Garber, Linda and Howard Reisman, Donna and Michael Weinstock, Norma and Peter Gordon, Viki and Paul Freeman, Rosemary and H. Jackson Brown Jr., Lori and Arthur Simon, Deedee Chereton, Lorie Lewis, Ava and Bob Wilensky, Cheryl and Phil Isaacs, Gail and Lyons Heyman, Shirley and Barry Retter, Carla and Ralph Lovell, Nancy and Wayne Freedman, Rabbi Arnold Goodman, Donna Taylor, Ashley Sparks, Tracy Green, Wendy Bowman-Littler, Sally Freedman, Janelle Nevins, Aleta Ellin, Diane Durham, Sally White, Philip Torres, Steve Aveson, Leslie Isenberg, Lisa Cohen, Elaine and Allan DeNiro, Jim Broadway, Monica Bernstein, Sherry Weinman and Michael Umanksy, Lee and Ed Reitman, Janet Schatten, John H. Hartley Jr., Peggy Roth, Karoline Brennan, Barbara Babbit Kaufman, Tim Hayes, Emery Pinter, the Direct Marketing Association, Ames Agami, Monique Gibson, Marshall Stowell, Aid Atlanta, Andrea Ross, Gina Wright, Evelyn Mims, Jill Becker, Bill Liss, Paige Trager, Melissa and Brad Sturm, The Lowe Gallery, Mark Shavin, Barron Segar, Arlene Hoffman, the Cohens, the Blonders, the Freedmans, Michelle Cumbo, Brennan Donnellan, Rick Frishman, Hillary Rivman, Planned Television Arts, and an endless array of friends, family members, readers, and viewers with whom I am blessed.

Preface

*W*hen I was a little girl, my father brought me home a cuddly brown teddy bear from a trip overseas. I recall hugging that bear with its button eyes and bright red bow around its neck. It was *the perfect present*. I loved that bear for a long time, because my father had picked it out *just for me*.

As an advocate of creative gift giving, I have always tried to give gifts that would really be adored and make a difference. The ideal outcome of the perfect present is that you make someone else feel remarkably special because you selected something just for them. The perfect present reflects their taste, not just yours. It is an expression of your heart that becomes a memory, often outlasting the gift itself. Because the perfect present really pleases someone, we learn that we gain so much when we give. Whoever said "It's better to give than to receive" understood the heartfelt feelings that come from giving *the perfect present*.

As the Super Shopper for over fifteen years on television, it's been my greatest pleasure to suggest gift ideas to millions of viewers. And over the years, as I've given gifts of my own, I've loved selecting presents that are tokens of my affection or friendship.

While the search for the perfect gift is one of my favorite things, you might be someone who dreads the task. But don't despair. We all need fresh ideas from time to time, and at one point or another we have all run out of time or energy, or been at a loss for finding the perfect gift!

As I researched this book, it became increasingly obvious that for centuries perfect presents have even become part of history—from the Statue of Liberty to the Taj Mahal. Kings to queens to heads of state— all have given gifts to bridge countries and cultures throughout the ages. In fact, gifts have been used to commemorate some of the greatest events in time, symbolizing freedom and peace.

You don't have to build monuments to express yourself, and giving that perfect present doesn't have to be a monumental task, either. But how do you choose the perfect present for someone you care about that will create a lasting impression and be treasured forever and ever?

Pursuing the Perfect Present

I wrote *The Perfect Present* with a lifetime of fabulous suggestions to help you select perfect presents for those individuals you care about. I also believe there is a clear distinction between an ordinary gift and a perfect present. While any gift is a token of your affection or appreciation, the perfect present is something that will endure through time and be totally memorable. Your entire personality is included in the present, and it illustrates great thought and concern for another's happiness.

Consider this book a present that's gift wrapped and ready to go. Filled with quick, creative ideas for every gift-giving occasion, it will serve as a valuable resource jam-packed with tried-and-true suggestions. Keep in mind, though, that the perfect present is more than a physical object; it's an extension of yourself. The perfect present signifies your feelings, an emotion, a moment in time, a thought.

Is there an art to giving the perfect present? Absolutely! To give the perfect present, you must make a match. For one person a poem is the perfect answer, for another it's the gift of time, and for another it's an heirloom a family member treasured for years. Everyone differs in their idea of the "perfect present."

Giving of ourselves is more important than giving what we have or are able to purchase. Add your feelings to a gift. As the final ingredient, write a note, a letter, or a card that sums up why you gave this gift. And don't forget that a big part of your present is your presentation. Every present should look too pretty to open!

To help you get organized for the perfect present, consider designating a special place in your home for gift wrap essentials. I dedicated a corner in a closet and found that a tall trash can was a wonderful holder for all of my supplies. Basics that I keep around include gift wrapping paper in a variety of themes and styles, spools of colorful ribbon, scissors, and a few rolls of clear tape. I also have a variety of personalized labels I keep in a drawer nearby, ready to stick on any package to let the recipient know the gift is from ME!

Whenever gift wrapping supplies are on sale, especially after the holidays, I love to stock up. Some years I buy up one particular style of paper good for any occasion, like a polka dot or a stripe, and use it year-round as my trademark. I also purchase various sizes and colors of gift bags with handles, which are great to have on hand for an instant gift wrap or in case an object has an unusual shape and is difficult to wrap.

And speaking of wrapping, don't forget to involve the kids! When our daughter, Ali, was ten, she learned to wrap a present and enjoyed it so much she literally wrapped everything in sight! Not only did she do a great job, but she received a great deal of satisfaction from a job well done.

When involving the kids, get creative and consider making your own wrapping paper. Kids love to make handprint paper with nontoxic paint in a variety of colors and a solid-colored paper like craft or drawing paper. You can also wrap a gift in plain white butcher paper and let the kids use their imaginations to decorate it. And don't forget your imagination, either! Add a little pizzazz to your package and attach a toy, ornament, or related object to the top of the gift when tying up the bow. When giving a book, add a bookmark on top, or tie a baby rattle to the bow on a gift for a newborn. Or consider giving your gift in a gift! Fill a colander with kitchen gadgets or a jewelry box with—you guessed it—something dazzling!

Timing Is Everything

And keep in mind one last gift-giving rule: No matter how excited you are about a gift . . . no gift should be given before it's time! Timing is everything, so make it part of the plan. The rewards? Seeing the joy in a child's eyes on his or her birthday, or your parent pleased with the one object he or she really needed—this perfect present will instantly boomerang right back to you in thank-yous and hugs!

As you search for the perfect gift, make it a meaningful journey. Choose your gifts with a thoughtful mind and a caring heart. Take great delight in the giving and your rewards will be heartfelt and plentiful. The thank-yous you receive in return will live on forever.

The Perfect Present Rules

✳ Promise little but then deliver big.

✳ Remember your previous gifts and be creative.

✳ Encourage a wish list. *Ask for ideas!*

✳ Start early, especially for big occasions.

✳ Explore and examine . . . what have they always wanted?

✳ Never plan on a return, but never, ever throw away a receipt.

✳ Try, try again, just in case. There's always next year!

Let the Shopping Begin!

The Perfect Present

Introduction: How to Choose the Perfect Present

When thou makest presents, let them be of such things
as will last long; to the end they may be in some sort immortal,
and may frequently refresh the memory of the receiver.
— THOMAS FULLER

Searching for the perfect gift? Think of gift giving as a secret mission. Your goal? To make someone else feel uniquely special and appreciated! To accomplish this, your gift must show thought, time, and some sort of conscious effort. Choosing the perfect present, a gift that someone will love, requires time and patience—whether that involves thinking long and hard about what you're going to give or spending all day searching for it.

The other secret to giving the perfect gift is to give something the person really wants or needs. One year your loved one might want an item for the house, and the next to be totally indulged with a gift just for them. Your job? Find out what people dear to you want . . .

the best gift ideas are discovered through a few carefully asked questions.

When in doubt, use the following Perfect Present Survey to investigate what the individuals on your gift-giving list would like.

The Perfect Present Survey

* ✳ What are some of your favorite presents you've ever received?
* ✳ What are some of your least favorite presents?
* ✳ What is your favorite color?
* ✳ What is your favorite flower?
* ✳ What is your favorite candy?
* ✳ What are your hobbies?
* ✳ What are your favorite foods?
* ✳ What is your favorite restaurant?
* ✳ What is your favorite perfume?
* ✳ Do you like receiving clothing as a present?
* ✳ Who is your favorite celebrity?
* ✳ Who is your favorite musician?
* ✳ What are the top five things on your wish list?

Once you know the answers to these questions, you should have a fairly good idea of what your friend or loved one likes and dislikes. You might even discover that you've been giving perfume all these years to someone who's allergic to it! If a person is shy about answering, then inquire often. You might be a fabulous mind reader, but some of the best gifts are the ones people really want and tell you about.

However, if you feel certain you're right on track, then use your intuition and go for it! And when you need a little help, use the ideas in this book to your heart's content! Count on *The Perfect Present* whenever there's a gift-giving emergency, and escape the gift-giving blues!

Create a Gift-Giving Calendar

Designate a generic calendar for your gift-giving list and get organized. Record everyone's birthday and other special days and use this calendar year to year as a constant reminder. My calendar sits on my office desk and reminds me when special events are coming up. During the first week of each month and as often as possible, I try to review whose birthdays or special days are coming up, presents I need to buy and wrap, cards I need to send, and more. I even keep a few presents such as toys, favorite books, or sweets on hand just in case of an emergency. You never know when you'll need a perfect present! Some months I'm so busy I find that it helps to preaddress envelopes ahead of time and even add a stamp. Planning is everything, so get ready!

Make a Match

While a toaster might be a perfect present for a kitchen-themed wedding shower, that doesn't mean it's the ideal gift for Valentine's Day. Choosing the perfect present takes time, effort, and insight, so be clever. Don't wait until the last moment to figure it out. Start early. Think about the person's likes and dislikes. Are they traditional or modern? What is their favorite color? Do they like simple things or fancy things? Plaid or polka dots? Cotton or silk? Do you have their actual sizes recorded? You never know when the perfect present will pop up!

The Finishing Touch: Deliver It in Style!

Whatever gift you select, think about the presentation and gift wrap as the finishing touch. The best gifts are delivered creatively. My husband, Willy, has always set a wonderful example for innovative gift giving. Once he gave me a bracelet in the head of a puppet. When I put the puppet on my hand I discovered the bracelet neatly tucked inside its head. And when we celebrated our twentieth wedding anniversary, he gave me a watch that was hidden in a compartment a seamstress had sewn into the back of a little teddy bear I had once admired.

So get busy! Whether you surprise someone with a note and a piece of yarn that has been strung throughout your entire house and they must follow the yarn to find the treasure, or whether you wrap the gift up and put it under their pillow, consider that *the perfect gift deserves a perfect arrival!*

On a Final Note:
What If the Perfect Present Is Sold Out or You Can't Locate It?

Sometimes the perfect present is so perfect, the entire world has purchased it before you can! This is especially common during the holidays, particularly with those hot toys or high-tech gadgets that have been heavily promoted all season long. Here are some helpful tips to help you locate those hard-to-find gifts:

✓ Call the store manager and ask when the item will be back in stock. Ask if the store is offering presales or creating a list in case the item is restocked. Get your name on the list, check often, and don't assume anything! Sometimes a store will save the items for a special ad they are running.

✓ Ask for a rain check. If you have a rain check, you have a better chance of getting the product at the advertised price when it comes in. It also helps to reserve one in your name. Make sure the store has all your telephone numbers!

✓ Shop early. Be the first to arrive at the store on special sale days. For example, the day after Thanksgiving, many stores open early and restock shelves with popular items. First come, first serve, and the early bird catches the present!

✓ Check with someone in another city. Ask a friend or relative to check in their city for the gift you are searching for. It might be sold out in one region of the country and readily available in another. You can also ask the store clerk to check the central office or other store locations for you.

✓ If the item is sold out, check your local newspaper's classified ads under "toys" and "miscellaneous" for special sales or resales of the item. Be absolutely certain to purchase the gift from a legitimate source, and if it's electronic, check to see that it works. Ask for a receipt of the sale no matter what.

✓ Call the manufacturer. Check to see if the manufacturer has a 1-800 number or a consumer hot line and phone to find out where they sell this item. You might find a new source that carries it. Sometimes you'll find popular toys at drugstores or other off-the-beaten-path retail outlets.

✓ Check catalogs. Many catalogs have a good stock of popular toys and gifts, even after the retail stores run out. Use the catalog's toll-free number and make sure they have the item in stock before you order it. Be sure to ask what happens if they are out of it. You might wish to back-order it and give the picture of the gift with a card to indicate it's on its way. Be sure to ask how long it will take for the gift to arrive. If it's the perfect present, it's worth waiting for!

✓ Try the Internet. Type in the name of your item and run a search to see if anyone has the item in stock. Make sure you know what you're getting by purchasing from a reliable source, and be a smart consumer.

✓ Check out fairs and flea markets. Often you'll find just the item you are looking for at a weekend flea market or garage sale. Check the newspaper for leads and events happening in your area where you could find gifts. You'll be surprised by how many other outlets you might discover, especially during the holiday season.

A Word to the Wise: Stay Focused

No matter what it takes, keep your focus. Never lose sight of the fact that the perfect present takes time and energy to find. The good news? The search is worth every second you spend, but just in case what you ordered isn't so perfect when it arrives, save your receipts, order forms, and all purchasing information for a prompt return. Be aware of exchange or return policies, and get the facts to ensure a positive experience, especially when ordering from a catalog or when cybershopping. And just in case you can't find the exact item you've been looking for, all you have to do is read this book to discover an endless source of perfect presents. Happy shopping!

Birthday Presents 1

*A*s the years have passed, birthdays have taken on new meaning. I always loved my birthday, but now I count my blessings every year and feel quite fortunate to grow older. I've learned, however, that birthdays are as much for everyone else who loves you as they are for you. I've also learned that it's important to be a gracious recipient of all that attention and show your appreciation.

One of my favorite birthdays of all time was when my friends kidnapped me for an entire day and surprised me with a shopping trip to an outlet center in Chattanooga, Tennessee, two hours away. We had an absolute blast, shopped until we dropped, and headed back home by dinnertime. My friends packed the car with snacks, and we all enjoyed spending a fabulous day together bargain shopping, something my busy schedule doesn't often permit. It took an army of friends with a strategic plan to coordinate this day for me, and talk about the perfect present—I loved every second of it!

While you don't have to kidnap someone and surprise them with a day away from home, you can make every birthday special and memorable. The element of surprise seems to be one of the secrets to the perfect present. And accomplishing that usually takes quite an effort, but it's worth every second. When I asked my mother what her favorite birthday present was, she immediately said it was the surprise luncheon we gave for her at our house on her sixtieth birthday. I was so glad I asked, because now I know that she loves surprises most of all.

The following ideas are birthday suggestions that have been treasured throughout the generations and make growing older something very special to look forward to each year.

FIFTIETH BIRTHDAY—FIFTIETH STATE! Each state in our country is listed in order of its admittance to the Union. On a special birthday, consider giving a surprise visit to the state that coordinates with the birthday honoree's age. Here are some favorites:

↩ HAWAII (#50): Make turning fifty a tropical breeze! Celebrate the big 5-0 in the fiftieth state . . . *aloha!*

↩ NEW YORK (#11): The Big Apple for an eleventh or any other big birthday! List eleven things you'll do when you get there!

↩ FLORIDA (#27): Here's a Mickey Mouse idea! Disney World's perfect for kids of all ages!

↩ CALIFORNIA (#31): Give a "California Dreamin'" birthday! Rodeo Drive, here we come!

↩ NEVADA (#36): The perfect birthday gift for high rollers . . . bet you'll have a great time!

COLLECTION PERFECTION. A wonderful birthday gift that has staying power is a starter collection for someone. Consider a theme or item that would be meaningful to them and build on it. Accompany your gift with a book that educates them about the object. From Limoges boxes in a variety of themes to magnificent paperweights, each year you can add one more. Over the years your gifts will grow in meaning and value. This also works well with gold beads or pearls—you can add one every year, and by the time a girl is twenty-one, the strand will be completed.

HAPPY BIRTHDAY TO THE BIG CHEESE. Call 1-800-ELI-CAKE (999-8300) and order one of the world's best cheesecakes from Eli's Cheesecake Company, in Chicago. These cheesecakes come in assorted flavors, including Chicago's Finest (Original Plain), Chocolate Chip, Candy Bar Cheesecake, Peanut Butter Blast, Chocolate Caramel Cluster Buster, and you can even order the Original Sampler if you can't make up your mind! Inquire about Eli's Cheesecake Club for monthly deliveries. (Prices begin at $25.00 plus delivery charge.)

THREE'S A CHARM. One of my favorite ways to make sure someone loves a gift is to go shopping and preselect three items for them. On their birthday, take them on a treasure hunt offering one of the three items. They'll get to select the one they love most, and you'll be thanked for all of your time and effort!

YOUNG AT HEART . . . BUT OLD ENOUGH TO BE AN AARP MEMBER? Call 1-800-424-3410 and purchase a membership to the American Association of Retired Persons (AARP). This gift is ideal for any birthday girl or boy who's turning fifty years or older. A yearly subscription costs about $8.00 a year per couple, but you can purchase a three-year membership that includes *Modern Maturity* magazine, the AARP bulletin, educational publications, and other special discount rates and services.

A PRESIDENTIAL GREETING. The White House Greetings Office of the President of the United States is standing by, ready to send an official birthday card to anyone eighty years old or older. Send your request in writing with the birthday girl or boy's name, address, and birth date, including the year, six weeks in advance to:

The Greetings Office
Room 39
The White House
Washington, D.C. 20500

WHO'S COUNTING? No matter how old the person is, take their age and write that many reasons why they are absolutely wonderful. Every year commands a compliment, so get busy. For instance, if someone's forty-five, you'll list forty-five things that you really adore about them. Go the extra mile and type it up and frame it! You could also give them forty-five chocolate kisses. Or try forty-five flowers, packs of gum, or the novelty of your choice to make your point.

BLOOMIN' GREAT GIFTS! Want to shop until you drop and stay home to boot? Call 1-800-777-0000 and order the Bloomingdale's by Mail, Ltd., catalog. It's filled with internationally renowned fashions and exclusive home designs, and jam-packed with gifts sure to delight.

MAKING HEADLINES. Here's a great birthday gift, especially as someone gets older! Call Historic Newspaper Archives at 1-800-221-3221, and order an original newspaper from any of fifty major U.S. cities, dating back from 1880 to the present. Give a specific birth date and ask them to send a newspaper published on that day, for $39.50 plus shipping and handling. Your gift includes a clear protective cover and a certificate of authenticity. Other custom presentations that are available for an additional charge include gold-leaf frames, bound books, or a personalized case with the recipient's name embossed in gold letters.

MAY YOUR CUP RUNNETH OVER! That's the perfect message to add to a gift sent from Starbucks Coffee Company. Call 1-800-STARBUC and order the finest-quality coffee, coffeemaking equipment, accessories, and confections. Overnight mail delivery, free gift cards, and gift certificates are available.

1-800-SEND-A-SONG. Looking for a creative way to say happy birthday? Send a song via the telephone to someone special with your own personalized, prerecorded, twenty-second message. Call 1-800-SEND-A-SONG, and they will fax or mail you a list of songs. You can also sample and hear a few great suggestions. From "Young at Heart" to "Happy Birthday to You," there's a perfect song just awaiting your call. The price is about $9.95 for one song, or you can purchase a number of songs as a package and save. This service allows you to program the time your song will be sent, and the choices are endless.

MUSIC TO THEIR EARS. Okay, so they're no longer a spring chicken. They'll still love a selection of music from the year they turned sweet sixteen. Calculate the years, and visit your local music store, and check out what music was playing when they were just sixteen years old. You're bound to stir up some fond musical memories with a selection from the good ol' days!

SAY HAPPY BIRTHDAY IN CHOCOLATE. That's right! Order the Hershey's Gift Catalog by calling 1-800-4KISSES (454-7737), and send a personalized chocolate greeting card with the birthday girl or boy's name right on it! They'll literally eat up this clever gift, and think you spent days searching for it. This catalog is also filled with a sweet selection of perfect presents for any chocolate lover on your list.

BIRTHSTONES GALORE! Call 1-800-BIRTHSTONES and check out the fabulous selection of birthstone jewelry available for every month of the year. The folklore associated with the tradition of the birthstone is that these gemstones bring good luck and protection. For over thirty-eight years, Saxe 800 Birthstones has specialized in custom jewelry incorporating your choice of birthstones. Bracelets, earrings, pins, necklaces, and more are all available with birthstones in a variety of shapes and sizes. Popular items include children's and grandchildren's birthstones incorporated into bracelets or pins for moms and grandmothers, and birthstone rings are also a huge hit. Here's a list of birthday months and their matching birthstones.

MONTH	COLOR	STONE
January	dark red	garnet
February	purple	amethyst
March	pale blue	aquamarine
April	white (clear)	diamond
May	bright green	emerald
June	cream	pearl or moonstone
July	red	ruby
August	pale green	peridot
September	deep blue	sapphire
October	variegated	opal or tourmaline
November	yellow	topaz or citrine
December	sky blue	turquoise or blue topaz

PRESERVE THE PAST. On my fortieth birthday, my mother made me a scrapbook that chronicled just about everything I had done since childhood. She had saved newspaper articles, photographs, and everything you could imagine and arranged it beautifully. She picked up where my baby books left off and presented me with a wonderful book filled with love and wishes for many more years of happiness.

YABBA DABBA DO! CALL ADLER & COMPANY. This fine art and animation gallery is dedicated to helping its clients build important collections. They offer a selection of vintage and contemporary production animation from all studios. They have clients who love hippos, clients who want dinosaurs, and clients who collect only first-season *Flintstones* pieces. Do some checking and find out what your birthday boy or girl's favorite cartoon was when he or she was younger and surprise him or her with a nostalgic blast from the past! Adler & Company also represents fine art, including "Britto interprets Disney." Call Adler & Company at 1-800-647-8007 and get creative with your gift giving!

A PIECE OF CAKE. They take the cake . . . anywhere! Since 1985, Piece of Cake has been baking gourmet cakes from scratch, wrapping them beautifully, and delivering them to customers' doors. Each cake is carefully made from scratch with only the finest all-natural ingredients. Ask about their fabulous assortment of gourmet pound cakes, perfect for sending long distance—from white chocolate pound cakes to luscious lemon pound cakes with lemon glaze frosting to chocolate chip pound cakes, you'll find this company will definitely take the cake. Two-day delivery is available. Call 1-800-9-CAKE-90 or 404-351-CAKE (local Atlanta).

1-800-BIRTHDAY! Call 1-800-BIRTHDAY and request a catalog or immediately order a present from America's birthday experts. This company is dedicated to helping busy people remember birthdays and select and send great birthday presents to anyone, at any time, anywhere across the country. Check out their custom-written Birthday Grams, performed live on the telephone and supplemented with delivery of keepsake lyrics, and you'll love sending their flowers and balloons, autographed sports memorabilia, toys for kids, and amazing edible presents. From bagels to birthday cakes, there's something for everyone! They have searched out the most innovative and fun-to-receive presents on the market. They also have a free Birthday Bank

Service so that you will never forget another important birthday again. You can register up to six important birthdays, and five to ten days prior to each of the dates registered, their birthday counselors will call you with a friendly reminder! Check out their Web site at 1-800birthday.com.

SONGS-4-U. Call 1-800-447-3708 and order a song from Songs-4-U, a company that specializes in writing and recording personalized songs for any occasion. Fill out their song questionnaire and specify anything you wish to be included in your song. They'll send you or your birthday boy or girl the customized song on a cassette.

A PICTURE'S WORTH A THOUSAND WORDS. Search for the perfect picture from someone's childhood and have it duplicated and enlarged. This will take a little investigating, but with a call to a family member you might find a wonderful memory that you can preserve forever. Consider a picture from when the person was little or a photo of them with a special family member. You could also have a photograph restored or colorized and present it in a frame, good as new!

Kids' Presents

A love of gifts begins at a very young age. Think back to your own childhood. Can you recall a time when you received a gift that was special—exactly what you wanted? Perhaps it was a bicycle, a puppy, or a piece of jewelry with your name on it. Maybe it was a brand-new teddy bear you loved until it was threadbare and barely stuffed. Some gifts just have a way of becoming embedded in your memory and heart forever.

Gifts that show thought and concern for a child's happiness are always remembered. Whatever the gift, it becomes an indelible memory that lasts forever. There are many different types of gifts that are far more precious than the latest gizmo on the market. Consider your presence as the greatest present of all. Gifts of time and togetherness can be the best gifts ever offered. You can also give the gift of a new skill, and some gifts offer an even bigger message that will be treasured for a lifetime. So, consider all the possibilities when giving a child a gift. What do you really want to accomplish?

While there are many gifts that will please a child, consider giving gifts that will have meaning long after they are given. If you can't find a specific gift a child really wants, consider a rain check, or in the case that you can't afford it, be honest and prepare your child ahead of time that he or she might not get the dream train set or porcelain doll.

The following are some wonderful examples of perfect birthday presents for children. They are also great gifts to give during the holidays and on other special days you wish to celebrate.

ONCE UPON A BOOK. From fairy tales to autobiographies, there's a perfect book for every child on your gift list. Consult with your local library or bookstore and match up a book for that child's age, or call 1-800-776-2242 and order a copy of Chinaberry, a special catalog filled with a wonderful selection of books for children and reviews of each book. When possible, make time to read the book to the child, or let the child read it to you! Older children love book series, so get started on a complete set. Give the first book with bookends and inscribe each book with a special saying. For little ones you might write, "When you read this book consider this: I filled each page with a hug and a kiss."

For older kids, "Remember this with every book I send: A book will be your lifelong friend."

AISLES OF SMILES. This gift never fails and is a surefire hit with kids of all ages. On the morning of the special day, surprise the child with a shopping spree to a favorite store. Designate a budget and watch the smiles as you cruise the aisles. This is an unhurried shopping excursion, so plan on at least a few hours to accomplish the mission. You'll probably see every toy or outfit in town, but rest assured your birthday boy or girl will thank you for buying exactly what he or she wanted!

STOCK UP! Here's one gift that will be appreciated and possibly even appreciate itself over time. For a child you will be giving a gift to every year, consider purchasing a stock that will grow with the child. Your pint-sized portfolio might turn out to be the best investment ever! As each year goes by, purchase that many shares of stock in a company the child might relate to. For example, when a child is one, buy one share of stock. A friend gave our son a share of Disney when he was born. The enclosed card said: "It's a small world, after all!" To make this even more fun, as the child gets older, let him or her help you select the stock. You'll be amazed how stock-smart kids can be, and they'll love choosing from the manufacturer of a favorite cereal, candy, or toy. . . .

THE SKY'S THE LIMIT. For that special child on your list who shines all year long, here's a gift that is heaven-sent. Call 1-800-528-STAR (7827) or 1-800-544-8814, and for $55.90 the Ministry of Federal Star Registration will match the child's name to a visible star that has never officially been named before. That star will be named after the child forever. The name and special occasion date you select will then be copyrighted in a book that is preserved in a federal government archive in Washington, D.C. In addition, the child will receive an eleven-by-seventeen-inch full-color certificate of record with the star's name, two sky charts identifying its location, a gift card with your personalized message, and a letter of congratulations signed by the registrar, briefly explaining how to telescopically locate the newly named star. Allow fourteen to twenty-one days for delivery.

HOW ABOUT ANIMAZING GIFT? Call 1-800-303-4848 and order the Animazing Gallery catalog. You'll find a huge selection of animation art. All artwork comes with a certificate of authenticity, and for a reasonable charge they will also mat and frame your selection. This gallery specializes in vintage cels, drawings, and limited editions from all studios. Just name the favorite cartoon character of the child on your gift list, and you'll be surprised at the fabulous choices that are available. Check out www.animazing.com for a closer look.

OH, POOH! Here's one of my favorite gifts to send a birthday girl or boy. Call 1-800-840-POOH and send a personalized Pooh Gram™ from Disney. They'll monogram the child's name right on Winnie the Pooh's outfit, and the cutest plush Pooh Bear you've ever seen will arrive at the little one's door. Dressed for the occasion, Pooh's ready for a party. Any birthday boy or girl will grin and bear a smile when they open up this adorable present. Disney's Pooh Grams™ can be ordered twenty-four hours a day, seven days a week and are available dressed for almost every holiday season and reason, including the arrival of a newborn. This gift is absolutely Pooh-fect . . . everyone will adore it! Only $29.95 plus shipping and handling.

THAT'S NOT ALL, FOLKS! Call 1-800-223-6524 and order a Warner Bros. Studio Stores catalog filled with fabulous gifts for kids of all ages. Warner Bros. has captured the magic of movies, television, and animated films and made it accessible to an international audience of shoppers. The catalog offers a wide array of merchandise for children and adults, featuring the popular Looney Tunes characters, DC Comics superheroes, and Cartoon Network characters. You'll find great gift-giving ideas for every price range, from Fred Flintstone Pez dispensers to Scooby Doo, Batman, and Sylvester T-shirts to cookie jars, toys, games, and limited-edition animated art. The Web site address is www.studiostore.warnerbros.com.

HUSH IS THE WORD! Choose a date for a secret outing and surprise your kids with a mystery trip. Don't tell them where you are going, and pack their stuff while they're asleep the night before.

Whether it's a trip to Disneyland or Disney World or to a city they've never visited before, the element of surprise will be treasured forever.

THEY'LL EAT THIS GIFT UP! For kids who are smart cookies and love an edible gift, call 1-800-435-6877 and order a Blooming Cookies catalog. It's filled with fabulous cookie presentations, and you'll find a special section dedicated to gifts for kids. They'll personalize a selection of creative containers, including favorite cartoon characters or dinosaurs, wagons, and more and then fill them with delicious cookies.

KIDS SAY THE FUNNIEST THINGS! Here's an idea I've used for each of our children. Purchase a blank book, and every time your child does or says something really cute or funny, write it down. Add your feelings and on your child's birthday write a letter in the book expressing your feelings about the year that has passed. Share this book with your child throughout the years. Here's a sample from our eleven-year-old daughter, Ali's, book when she was four: "Mommy, I really feel sick. If you don't believe me, you can ask God!"

SHAKE IT UP BABY! Snow domes are a favorite toy adored by children of all ages, and they can be found for all budgets. From specialty stores to gift stores at airports, you'll find them all over. Consider giving a special snow dome on each birthday, and then all year long if you travel or visit a new city, bring one back. Over the years your child will love hearing stories about where each snow dome came from, and the whole family can join in as they begin to take their own trips. Write a special message at the bottom.

WHAT A DOLL! Call 1-800-845-0005 and order the American Girl's Collection catalog from Pleasant Company for a magnificent selection of the prettiest dolls and accessories you've ever seen. They even have matching outfits for your living doll, as well as books about the dolls and their adventures. There's even a doll hospital available for dolls that have been loved to pieces. These dolls are the perfect gift for your perfectly precious child!

HAPPY CAMPERS. Kids at camp? Call 1-800-736-3998 and order a "Thinking of You" Summer Camp Surprise Package from The Wrinkled Egg.® Each package is individually tailored to the specific interests of your favorite camper. The Wrinkled Egg® offers nearly nine hundred different fun, exciting, and kid-friendly items. Autographed pillowcases, magic tricks, trinkets, Frisbees, footballs, pocket games—just name it and it will be packaged up in a fabulous presentation and shipped ASAP. Packages are sent daily Monday through Saturday, and during the summer the company is open seven days a week. Count on this as a great resource all year long for every kid occasion imaginable.

CALLING ALL KIDS. Call 1-800-285-5555 and order a catalog from Lilly's Kids that is filled with a wonderful assortment of toys, imaginative costumes, games, crafts, and learning activities. Be sure to check out the personalized items. A guaranteed winner!

SEALED WITH A KISS. Call 1-800-888-SWAK and check out the Super Camp Care Packages® from a company called Sealed With A Kiss.® The packages are filled with the trendiest games, toys, puzzles, plush animals, cool stuff for teens, and an endless array of fun presents for boys and girls ages five through twenty. They also send gift packages for all occasions, including college, holidays, newborns, adults, travel packages, speedy recovery, "thinking of you," and more. Sealed With A Kiss® searches the world for their products and creates themed packages for all occasions. They have been featured on *Oprah!* Check out their web site at www.swakpack.com.

FIRST SET OF WHEELS. For a perfect birthday gift, surprise a child with that fabulous bicycle he or she has been wanting. Take your child with you for a perfect fit, and then on the special day have the bike assembled and waiting at the front door wrapped in a bright red ribbon! Be sure to include a properly fitted bicycle helmet and supervised lessons for learning to ride safely!

PLUGGED IN! Ask any preteen or teenager what he or she wants for a birthday present and most will request a computer, a private telephone or phone line, the latest video game system, or a personal television set. If you aren't the teen's parent, get parental approval first. Get the facts before purchasing electronic equipment, and make sure it can be returned or exchanged. If you choose a telephone, get it installed while the child is at school and then surprise him or her by plugging it in during the night and waking him or her up with a birthday-morning telephone call! If it's a television set or a computer, surprise the recipient by having it ready for immediate use. Be sure to investigate which cable hookups or electrical outlets are needed ahead of time. No delayed gratification here!

WHAT A JEWEL! If you give a child a piece of jewelry on a special birthday, create a unique delivery by being imaginative. Consider putting earrings on a stuffed animal that has soft ears that you can easily pierce, or hang a necklace around a doll that resembles the child. You could even borrow one of the child's own stuffed toys.

CALL DISNEY! The Disney catalog, which is published eighteen times a year, offers more than six hundred quality Disney products and gifts, including toys, apparel, collectibles, and housewares, for every member of the family. Special once-in-a-lifetime Disney gift packages, ranging from private Disneyland parties to VIP visits with the Mighty Ducks of Anaheim, are offered once a year in the holiday issue. Call 1-800-237-5751 to place an order or receive a free subscription to the Disney catalog. Or check out the Web site at www.disneystore.com.

LOOK-ALIKES! Call 1-800-469-8946 and order the My Twinn catalog. You'll find a unique company that specializes in one-of-a-kind dolls that will be personalized to look like your child.

Shower, Wedding, and Anniversary Presents

3

*F*rom shower to wedding to anniversary presents, gifts for newlyweds or even seasoned couples are often hard to choose. When selecting a gift for the bride and groom, my best advice is to inquire about where they registered. Newlyweds are often inundated with gifts, so make sure yours is something they really want and will treasure.

When it comes to anniversary gifts, it's important to choose something the couple will enjoy. The following ideas will help you select a perfect present, but keep in mind that what's perfect for one couple may not be for another. Check with someone who knows what the pair might want, or ask the couple what they need and will appreciate over time. Almost every couple now registers with a computerized registry, and with mail-order options available, it's simple to locate the perfect present. The best gifts are the ones that people really use (they may already have three fondue sets), so do some homework before making your purchase.

Wedding Showers

SHOWER THE BRIDE AND GROOM WITH YOUR AFFECTION. From bath towels to washcloths and all kinds of shower accessories, here's a great way to shower the bride and groom with love! Lather up a gift that will be perfectly suited for the master bath and monogram some towels as his and hers.

KITCHEN SHOWER. Help the couple get ready to cook up something special in the kitchen. Fill a colander with kitchen gadgets—from the best bottle opener to measuring spoons to a garlic press. These gifts will really be put to use!

FIT TO BE TIED. For any couple about to tie the knot, give them an assortment of gift wrapping paper and ribbon. Add a personal touch by calling Personal Creations at 1-800-326-6626 and ordering from their unique catalog of customized items, which includes ribbon with the bride and groom's names on it and the wedding date stamped in gold or silver, plus many other surprises. This creative gift will come in handy all year long.

Wedding

WHAT GIFT WILL REGISTER? Brides and grooms commonly register for items they really want. Ask the bride and groom or a family member or friend where they have registered, and check out their wish list. The answer for the perfect present will be a telephone call away, so don't try and reinvent the wheel on this one!

A BOUQUET THAT NEVER WILTS. For many a bride, parting with the beautiful flowers she carried down the aisle is sweet sorrow. Give her the gift of those lovely blooms forever—have the bouquet recreated in silk flowers! Talk to the florist who did the wedding about a silk bouquet, or take a good close-up photograph of the bouquet to someone who specializes in silk stems. (If it's to be a surprise, bring your camera along to the reception and take your own shot of the bouquet rather than asking the bride for one.) Or if silk flowers aren't her style, enlarge the photograph taken of the bouquet and frame the picture. And last but not least, consult with her florist and discuss resources for having her bouquet dried and preserved immediately following the wedding. Once the process is completed, the bouquet can be framed for lasting beauty.

A PLACE TO KEEP MEMORIES. Give the sentimental bride a keepsake box where the couple can keep mementos from their wedding day. If you enjoy giving it your creative touch, you could make one yourself by choosing a hatbox or an unfinished wooden box about the size of a shoe box. Finish it with decoupage, paint, or a cover of lace and satin. Perhaps label it "Wedding Memories" and add the date of the wedding. Or purchase an attractive keepsake box, made of anything from a smoothly finished exotic wood to beveled glass. Consider having a small plaque engraved with the couple's name and wedding date affixed to the box.

INVITATION SENSATION. Check out the bridal department at any store that specializes in wedding presents, or visit a store that does engraving, and search for a way to creatively reflect the couple's wedding invitation and preserve it creatively. It's never too late to give this present, especially if a bride and groom never received one as a gift. You could have the wedding invitation engraved on a crystal or silver box. Your gift will definitely be appreciated for years to come.

FILLED TO THE BRIM WITH HAPPINESS. A beautiful crystal pitcher will always be appreciated, so consider selecting one and add a note that says, "May your life together be filled to the brim with happiness!"

TIMELESS TREASURES. Call 1-800-526-0649 and request the Tiffany & Co. catalog. When that signature blue box arrives filled with gorgeous gifts for the bride and groom, they'll not only cherish your gift, but they'll save the box, too! You'll find a beautiful selection of crystal, silver, china, vases, and stunning accessories that will be treasured for a lifetime. Tiffany & Co. is definitely one of my favorite places for gifts that will be remembered forever and ever.

PICTURE PERFECT. Save the wedding invitation and have it framed in a beautiful silver frame or another frame that's really special. Not only will the couple appreciate your gift, but over the years they will look back and appreciate your thoughtful keepsake.

PERFECT FROM THE START. Friend of both sides of the family? Here's a nostalgic and creative idea. Borrow photographs of the bride and groom when they were just babies and have copies made. Return the originals and have your copies framed together. Add a note with your gift that says, "May your love grow through the years as beautifully as you both have!"

BREAK TRADITION. Have a Jewish bride and groom on your gift list? Call 1-800-729-2321 and give the couple The Lucite® Wedding Cube from the Treasured Collection. Send the actual broken glass or bulb from the ceremony, and the Treasured Collection will have it suspended in a clear cube with the couple's name and wedding date embossed on the case. They'll also suspend in a Lucite® Cube the wedding or any other kind of invitation you want to present as a keepsake. Talk about the perfect present; this is the ultimate one-of-a-kind gift that will be treasured forever.

A STERLING IDEA. Call 1-800-262-3134 and order the Silver Queen catalog. The catalog is filled with current patterns, and Silver Queen will also help you find a special piece you've been searching for. Silver Queen specializes in the replacement of hard-to-find sterling silver flatware and has over 1500 patterns in stock, both new and estate. Check out their bridal registry and their assortment of beautiful silver wedding gifts. A helpful resource for years to come!

CLEARLY A PERFECT GIFT! When I got married twenty-two years ago, my husband and I received a Steuben bowl. It's still one of my favorite wedding gifts and a magnificent treasure we continue to love. For nearly one hundred years, the glassmakers, designers, engravers, and polishers at Steuben have created elegant functional objects and sculptural art of timeless beauty. Whether you give a piece just from you or coordinate a group gift, Steuben is an ideal resource for the perfect present. Call 1-800-424-4240 and order the Steuben catalog to choose from America's finest glass vases, bowls, animals, paperweights, and sculptures.

Anniversary Gifts

SHOW HOW MUCH YOU LOVE HER. If a trip to Broadway is out of the question, how about tickets to a touring production of a popular show? It'd be great to get them for the day of your anniversary or for that of someone you love, but even if that's not possible, present the tickets with a note that says, "I'm glad you're my leading lady (or man)," or, "Here's a gift to 'show' how much I (we) love you!"

A TOKEN FROM YOUR HEART. Hearts come in all shapes and sizes, from diamond hearts to crystal heart-shaped paperweights, and even chocolate ones. Regardless of your budget or the type of heart you choose, add a thoughtful note that says, "Here's a gift straight from my heart. May we never, ever be apart."

GIVE TRADITION A TWIST. You've probably seen those lists of "traditional anniversary gifts" that name appropriate types of presents, such as paper and glass, to give for certain anniversaries. Well, use that as a starting point. For example, the traditional first anniversary gift is made of paper. How about airline tickets? The fifth anniversary is wood—a piece of antique furniture would be nice. The eleventh anniversary is steel—a new car would be cause for celebration!

FOR A PERFECT PAIR. Call Harry and David at 1-800-547-3033 and consider sending the anniversary couple a box of pears! Order their spectacular catalog filled with a fabulous assortment of fruit and packaged gifts. Their pears are absolutely delicious, and so big and juicy you can eat them with a spoon. Add a note saying, "We're glad you two paired up!" or, "To a perfect pair . . . Happy Anniversary!"

THEY'RE PLAYING OUR SONG. What kind of music did you and your mate listen to when you were dating? Buy some compact discs or put together a tape of favorite songs from those days. Include a note that says, "I still hear music when I think of you." Or, call 1-800-227-2190 and check out the endless selection of music boxes available from the San Francisco Music Box Company catalog. Consider ordering a music box playing the song you walked down the aisle to or the music played during your first dance at your wedding.

IT WAS A VERY GOOD YEAR. Having a difficult time selecting an anniversary gift? Here's an idea that will help you celebrate the couple's years of marriage. Select a bottle of wine from the year the couple was married and toast their anniversary with a vintage gift. You can also add wineglasses or a wine-bottle opener for a festive touch. *Special note:* Check with a wine steward or maître d' to make sure the older vintages are still drinkable and in their prime. Certain varieties taste like vinegar after a couple of years.

Baby Presents 4

When a baby is born, it's one of the most exciting moments in the parents' lives. It also seems to require an army of equipment, supplies, gadgets, and gizmos to bring baby home. With choices from strollers to infant carriers to blankets to bottles, deciding what to give baby shouldn't be a huge problem or cost a bundle. Baby gifts are among the most fun to give, since a baby needs absolutely everything. And even if they don't need it, baby gifts are so adorable they're almost impossible not to appreciate.

Common goals when purchasing a gift for a baby are finding something that will really be useful or something that will be long remembered and treasured. If the parents really need functional objects, stick to the practical. If it seems like the baby will be deluged with gifts, go for the most creative and imaginative ideas you can think of.

 To this day one of my favorite gifts was my first baby dress, which my mother had saved for years and

then gave to me. It was the same one I wore in a baby picture that sat framed on her bureau. That dress is now hanging in our daughter, Ali's, room in a beautiful frame, right next to Ali's first dress in a matching frame. And talk about sentimental: I saved baby clothes Ali wore as an infant and had a quilter cut them up and incorporate them into a quilt for her bed and also a magnificent wall hanging that is proudly displayed in her room. I even have a storage box for both of our children, filled with toys, gifts, and cards they received when they were born. Perhaps someone saved some special item that was yours when you were an infant and can be passed down and worn at a baby naming.

The following gifts range from creative to sentimental to totally practical. With a little homework you can select the perfect present for a baby that will delight everyone. Here are some wonderful ideas to get you started!

YOUR DAY IN HISTORY. Frame the front page of a newspaper from the day the baby was born, or preserve the entire paper in a photo storage box (available at photo shops, office supply stores, and some craft shops). If the family has long ties to the community, you might want to use the hometown paper. For a more global view of what the world was like the day the baby entered it, visit a newsstand and purchase a copy of *USA Today*, the *New York Times*, or some other paper that covers national and world news. When the child is old enough to read and study history, the newspaper will be an instant reference as to what life was like the day he or she arrived.

A TIMELESS TOY. Grandparents and older aunts and uncles can think back to when the new parents were infants. What was the parent's favorite toy when he or she was tiny? Most likely, it was a classic that is still available, and the new member of the family will enjoy playing with the toy as much as his mom or dad did.

START BABY'S BOOK NOOK. Babies are interested in books at a surprisingly early age. They especially love books with simple pictures, books with flaps they can lift, and activity books, which appeal to many of their senses. Buy several sturdy cardboard books or cloth/vinyl books that a baby can thumb through alone or have read to them. For a classic storybook, how about *Goodnight Moon* by Margaret Wise Brown? Another classic, *Pat the Bunny,* by Dorothy Kunhardt, will keep little hands busy with a variety of activities.

IF THE SHOE FITS. Call 1-800-543-8566 and order a free catalog from the Livonia Collection. This company offers a unique and beautiful selection of personalized leather baby shoes and other items for babies, including creatively wrapped themed gift packages. Everyone will get a kick out of your gift when they open it up and find baby's name and birth date custom-engraved on the sole of the shoes. If you want to send the gift before the baby actually arrives, the parents will receive a certificate that they can return when the baby is named so the shoes can be properly personalized. You can also visit their Web site at www.babyshoe.com.

MAKE A SPLASH WITH THIS GIFT! Purchase a portable infant tub and fill it with bath toys, rubber ducks, and colorful sponge toys. Throw in an infant towel and washcloth set. Both parents and baby will enjoy turning bath time into fun time. Add a note that says, "Splish splash, enjoy these with your bath!"

BE A REAL SWINGER. Babies love to swing, and parents love swings because they keep an infant quiet and happy for quite a while. Freestanding models come in windup and battery-powered versions—both are good for small babies. For babies older than six months or so, a child-safe swing that can be attached to a tree, deck, or other outdoor location is a gift that can be used (and loved) for years.

FIND A FAMILY HEIRLOOM. In some families, baby naming or christening gowns are kept for decades and used by every new member of the family. Other families have no such heirloom, but would cherish one even if it came from outside the family. Antique gowns can be found at some antiques stores, shops that specialize in vintage linens and apparel, and sometimes at flea markets. There is some serendipity involved in making the right find, so start your search early in order to have plenty of time to find this perfect present.

SAY IT WITH PEWTER. Call 1-800-222-3142 and order a catalog from Danforth Pewterers, which offers a variety of mementos for the new child, including a pewter cup, bowl, plate, and spoon. Prices range from $22.00 to $65.00, depending on the item, and all the pewterware can be engraved. While pewter looks elegant, it's quite durable and can take the abuse a growing child will give it.

A BASKET FOR BABY. Here's a fabulous baby shower or newborn gift for the baby who needs everything! Fill a basket with odds and ends—from bibs to books to safety gadgets, and all of your favorite things that baby will need. Add a poem that says:

> *Babies need a zillion things,*
> *This fact is definitely true.*
> *But this baby has the perfect present,*
> *A Mom and Dad like you!*

JUST FOR FUN. There's no doubt about it, you could fill a room with practical items a baby needs. But sometimes, it's more fun to choose a whimsical gift that will make you the showstopper at any baby shower. How about an off-the-wall gift? A baby-sized denim jacket, for example, and a tiny Hawaiian-print top and sunglasses to go with it. Or, baby's first cowboy boots or a monogrammed bathrobe would make a huge hit. A visit to the baby section of any major department or specialty store should yield some fun ideas.

A TREE-MENDOUS WELCOME. Plant your thought and give baby a tree sapling that can be planted in the family's yard. As the child grows, he or she will have fun watching "my birthday tree" grow and comparing his or her own height to that of the tree.

READY TO GO. Prepare a travel kit for baby. Get lots of travel-sized packs of diaper wipes, baby bath soap and lotion, and other toiletries and supplies baby will need on the road. In the hustle and bustle of preparing for those first trips with baby, Mom will be happy to have them handy. Purchase a diaper bag and have it monogrammed for an extra-special touch.

A GIFT YOU CAN'T BEAR TO BE WITHOUT! Call 1-800-829-BEAR (2327) and order the Vermont Teddy Bear Company™ catalog. This charming catalog is filled with bears of all descriptions and themes. Choose one of their baby bears. These bright baby-soft bears are squishy, squashy, and perfect for little hands. Their colorful clothing can be personalized with the new baby's name and this is a long-lasting gift that will be treasured for a lifetime.

THE DAY YOU WERE BORN. With all the commotion surrounding a baby's birth, parents often forget to save items from the day baby was born. Create your own sentimental gift by packing up the following objects: the front page of the newspaper, baby's horoscope from that day, the comics pages, and anything else you can think of. Now it's time to get really creative. Take a photograph of a beautiful flower that is in bloom that day and consider snapping pictures of other significant details like the weather or anything special that is happening on the day baby is born. If you visit the hospital, also take a picture of the building and any activities that seem pertinent, including family members gathered around the viewing room. This gift takes a little thought, but will be appreciated beyond words.

TWO TO GET READY. If the baby has a brother or sister who is still in a stroller, give a double stroller that seats two. Talk about perfect presents: this one is a total luxury, and also a necessity for the mom and dad who have two little ones to cart about.

PERSONALIZE IT. Putting baby's name on a gift is always appreciated. Call 1-800-264-6626 and order the Personal Creations catalog, which specializes in the cutest personalized items you've ever seen. You'll find a wide assortment of unique gifts that are perfect for baby, including accessories, toys . . . just name it!

THE NAME GAME. There are dozens of songs that are based on a variety of names. Visit your local sheet music store and check out the options. If you find one that fits the baby's name and the occasion, have it framed. You'll be surprised how many options are available, from "Danny Boy" to "Mandy."

CREATE A TOY COLLAGE. Transform a framed mirror, plastic clock, box, bulletin board, or picture frame into a creative work of art. Collect small toys, odds and ends, trinkets, or anything that relates to the theme of baby's room. Collage the objects around the border of the frame or item using a fast drying, permanent glue. Let dry, and with a little imagination you'll have a perfect present. For a special touch, include baby's name spelled out in plastic alphabet letters or beads.

Christmas and Kwanzaa Presents 5

*T*he holiday season is one of the most exciting and rewarding gift-giving occasions. Choosing the perfect present during the holidays, when you probably have a long list of gifts to buy, can be difficult. The secret? Start early and add the fun back into gift buying. When you wait until the last moment, finding the perfect present can be much more difficult and even stressful. So try to plan and prepare for making the most of your holiday gift giving.

However, if like most people you've waited until the last moment or are still at a loss for what to give, look no further. The following ideas run the gamut from inexpensive to the sky's the limit! Whatever your budget, keep in mind that you can find the perfect present even if money is totally the object! Go on a search for something that will be useful and practical, and think about what that person really enjoys or needs, from her favorite candy to his sport of choice. My motto: "Think first, buy later!"

Christmas

THE GIFT OF TOGETHERNESS. Pool the money you'd normally spend on individual gifts for your immediate family, and use it to pay for a family vacation. A trip to a ski area or beach resort will result in plenty of happy family memories that will last far longer than the usual toys, sweaters, and compact discs you'd normally give your kids. Make it a surprise, and instead of sitting by the tree all day, head to the airport.

THE GIFT OF TRADITION. Help your children to understand what's special and unique to your family by putting together a scrapbook for each child highlighting some of your family traditions. Include recipes you use for Christmas cookies and other foods you make only at Yuletide, stories about family traditions and how they began, and perhaps some photos taken at previous Christmases. You might want to leave room for your children to add their own thoughts and traditions each year.

INCREDIBLE EDIBLES FROM BALDUCCI'S. Call 1-800-225-3822 and order the fabulous Balducci's catalog, filled with an outstanding variety of edible gifts. For three generations the Balducci family has searched the world for the finest foods. From beef Wellington to lobster thermidor, from Mamma Balducci's Original Pasta Sauces to heavenly desserts, you'll find a spectacular selection of gourmet gifts in this terrific catalog. *Buon appetito!*

BREAKFAST WITH SANTA! Do you have a family on your list with young kids who will likely have their parents out of bed before daybreak on December 25 to open presents? Put a special surprise under their tree. Give them a basket filled with muffins, bagels, jams and jellies; maybe even some coffee beans, hot chocolate mix, and chocolate Santas for a breakfast dessert. That way, the exhausted parents don't have to worry about making breakfast for their overexcited youngsters. Enclose a note saying, "There's 'muffin' like being together for breakfast on Christmas morning!"

THE CHIMNEY WITH CARE. A Christmas stocking is a lifelong gift. Many adults still have the one their grandmother knitted for them when they were just toddlers, and it carries with it decades of memories. Present a special stocking to a child, or even an adult who doesn't have one. While hand-knit stockings are an old-time favorite, department and specialty stores, as well as catalogs, today offer a wide variety of attractive Christmas stockings, including needlepoint ones and other types that look like they are handmade. Stay away from trendy designs such as the latest movie, even for children—go for a classic theme that could last a lifetime. And remember, a stocking isn't really special until it has the recipient's name permanently affixed to it.

1-800-CELEBRATE. That's right! Dial that number and order the Celebration Fantastic catalog, which is totally devoted to celebrating whatever season is at hand. You'll love this gift catalog, which offers some of the most clever items you've ever seen and is jampacked with gifts of every theme and description. This is one of my favorites—don't even consider celebrating without it!

DELIVER DINNER! You can send dinner to someone's door by calling Omaha Steaks and ordering a gift box filled with steaks. Call 1-800-228-9055 for a gift they can really sink their teeth into. Or cook up one of your favorites, give fair warning, and deliver dinner in disposable containers. Give the cook a night off and your gift will definitely be a hit.

A GIFT THAT WILL HANG AROUND FOR YEARS. Many adults have a favorite Christmas tree ornament from childhood or focus on a particular theme each year to decorate their tree. Do some homework and give an ornamental gift that suits someone to a T. From personalized ornaments to collectibles to ornaments that remind them of their childhood, there's something for everyone. You could even start an ornament collection for a child and give one each year as a present, or creatively attach an ornament to top off their gift package.

SCENT OF THE SEASON. Don't you love the piney smell of a fresh Christmas tree? With more and more people using artificial trees, that woodsy odor is becoming rarer. Consider giving the cheerful scent of Christmas with something natural and beautiful, such as a handmade wreath or centerpiece. If you have the talent and supplies, you can make a gift yourself. Otherwise, visit garden shops, Christmas tree stands, church bazaars, and other seasonal shops to find ready-made items of pine, spruce, or mountain laurel. Wreath making is a seasonal cottage industry in some rural parts of the country, and you may find mail-order sources on the Internet.

I'LL BE HOME FOR CHRISTMAS. There's nothing like Christmas to remind someone that he or she is all alone and away from family. The best present in the world in this situation is a ticket for a plane, train, or bus that's homeward-bound. In the event that a trip is not possible, exchange videotapes filled with holiday sentiments and favorite past memories to be viewed on Christmas morning at the exact same time!

I'LL HAVE A BLUE CHRISTMAS WITHOUT YOU. Echo the words of the Elvis Presley tune with something blue to let your better half know how much you'll miss her. Sapphire jewelry is one possibility, but for something contemporary, consider lapis jewelry from the Sundance catalog (1-800-422-2770). The name of the semiprecious stone comes from the Arabic word for blue. Denim lapis—a soft blue like a familiar pair of jeans—is currently very popular. Sundance has everything from lapis rings and earrings to lapis-studded wristwatches and hair clamps.

GIVE SUGARDALE A CALL! Call 1-800-860-4267 and order gourmet meats, from turkeys to hams to steaks, from Sugardale Foods. Request a catalog for a super sampling of quality meats that make excellent gifts.

ALL IN THE FAMILY. Bring a family together by giving them a reason to get together. Give them the ingredients for a family game night! Wrap up a couple of board games that accommodate lots of people and require lots of interaction, such as Scrabble, Boggle, Jeopardy!, or Monopoly. Add some snacks to keep the energy level up, and they'll play late into the night.

SAY CHEESE. Call 1-800-798-2954 and order the Mozzarella Company catalog. Whether you want to wish the big cheese a Merry Christmas or know someone who is a cheese fanatic, they'll love a gift from the Mozarella Company. Since 1982, this company has produced award-winning handmade, gourmet cheeses. Inquire about their gift baskets and other cheese selections.

A HINT OF IRISH. There's an old Irish saying that if you're Irish you never go anywhere without one arm being shorter than the other. This obviously means that one arm is always loaded down with gifts! So in the spirit of the Irish, or if someone you wish to give a gift to is Irish, call 1-800-338-2085 and order the Irish Cottage catalog. Filled with Irish clothing and gifts, this is the perfect resource for that hard-to-please leprechaun on your list.

ETHEL M. CHOCOLATES. Call 1-800-4-EthelM and order an exquisite catalog filled with gift sets featuring outstanding chocolates. Forrest Mars founded the famous Mars candy company in honor of his mother, Ethel Mars. Choose from Almond Butter Krisps to their legendary Lemon Buttercreams, or even chocolate greeting cards. You can sweeten any occasion with beautifully wrapped fruit-shaped chocolates cradled in a variety of decorative gift boxes, including Victorian-style tin boxes and hand-painted porcelain teapots. There's something for every chocoholic! Try including a note that says, "Stay sweet."

GIVING BOTH WAYS. Global Crafts, the catalog from the Christian Children's Fund Craft Cooperative, features beautiful handmade items from around the world, including jewelry, textiles, hand-carved items, and native crafts. This source offers stunning arts and crafts the recipient will love, and the money you spend through this catalog will go to support impoverished children and families around the world. To receive a free catalog, call 1-800-366-5896.

HAVE AN ANGEL ON YOUR LIST? If you have an angel of a friend or someone who loves sweet temptations, here's the ideal resource. Call the De Brito Chocolate Factory at 1-800-588-3886 and order their catalog, which offers a cornucopia of heavenly chocolates and luscious fruits. Their Christmas presentation is wrapped in a box covered with cherubs and gold trim, and their "California's finest" apricots dipped in chocolate will put your gift at the top of anyone's list. Be sure to check out their California Gold Rush Bar, a super stocking stuffer for anyone with a heart of gold and a love of chocolate.

HALLMARK AT HOME. Call 1-800-983-4663 and order the Hallmark at Home catalog, filled with unique fine gifts and collectibles. From keepsake ornaments to holiday cassettes, there's something here for everyone on your shopping list.

CREATE A DRESS-UP KIT. Children love playing dress-up, so as a special gift for a child or a couple of siblings, present them with lots of fun clothes, hats, and costume jewelry. This doesn't have to be an expensive gift—weed out your own closet or visit a local thrift shop for items. Pick out a good variety of clothes, including formal wear, uniforms, and accessories such as shoes and junk jewelry. While you're at the thrift store, look for an old suitcase that can hold the dress-up kit and complete the theme.

THE WORD IS BYRD. Call 1 -800-291-BYRD and check out this catalog filled with gourmet award-winning sweet and savory snacks and cookies. This exclusive selection of gourmet products comes from the Byrd Cookie Company, established in 1924, which has annually baked millions of cookies that are totally scrumptious and mouthwatering.

HAPPILY EVER AFTER. Call 1-800-FAIRYTALE (324-7982) and order a complimentary catalog from Fairytale Brownies, or visit the gourmet brownie experts on-line at www.brownies.com. Check out their eleven heavenly flavors, including mint chocolate, raspberry swirl, and white chocolate chunk, for a brownie that's a legend in its own time.

SANTA SHOPS HERE! Call 1-800-343-3095 and order The Paragon, a whimsical gift catalog filled with a unique and creative assortment of fabulous gifts for everyone on your list, including dog, cat, and frog lovers. You'll also find decorative accessories, keepsakes, clever door mats, porcelain boxes, and more. There's something for everyone, just ask Santa!

Kwanzaa

Kwanzaa is a celebration of African-American culture observed from December 26 to January 1, and while gift giving is part of the tradition, commercialization is not. The name comes from the Swahili word *kwanza*, which means "first." It is part of the phrase *matunda ya kwanza*, which means "first fruits."

Kwanzaa presents should be affordable and have artistic or educational value. Creativity is one of the values celebrated by Kwanzaa, so making gifts is completely appropriate. If you choose to buy Kwanzaa gifts, look for beautiful and useful items made by African-American artists and craftspeople (available at craft fairs throughout the year).

A FAMILY AFFAIR. Check out the book *Kwanzaa: A Family Affair* by Mildred Pitts Walter (Avon Books, 1995). It is filled with a rich explanation of the history, symbols, and true meaning of this holiday. You'll also find suggestions for activities you and your family can do during Kwanzaa, including special crafts, recipes, games, and gifts to help make this celebration come to life in a meaningful way.

KWANZAA FUN. Another book that focuses on creative presents you can make is *Kwanzaa Fun: Great Things to Make and Do* by Linda Robertson and Julia Pearson (Kingfisher, New York, 1996). This book has a wonderful selection of things that you can do with children and is jam-packed with ideas and activities for bringing Kwanzaa to life while teaching children about the real meaning of the celebration.

Hanukkah Presents

6

*H*anukkah, the Festival of Lights, is a Jewish holiday that celebrates religious freedom. *Hanukkah* means "dedication," and the holiday commemorates the victory of the Maccabees over the Syrians. On the twenty-fifth day of Kislev, the Maccabees cleansed the Temple, which had been desecrated. To rededicate the Temple, holy oil was needed to light the Temple's menorah (candelabra). The Jews searched and searched but found only a small bit of oil, barely enough to last a day. Miraculously, the oil burned for eight days. During Hanukkah, gifts are exchanged over the course of eight days and a menorah is lit each night to symbolize the miracle that occurred.

When I think about all the Hanukkahs we've celebrated in my family, I realize that the best part is the family tradition of getting together. Latkes (traditional fried potato pancakes) are served with homade applesauce, and the musical menorah my Grandpa Irving gave my brother is lit, then turned on to play "Rock of Ages." We select names and exchange presents.

Perfect Hanukkah presents are discovered by asking the question, "What do you *really* want?" Everyone goes to great lengths to find something each cousin, aunt, uncle, and grandparent will really love. And there's always Aunt Francie or Grandma Pauline, who does not want a thing! But we try our best anyway, and sometimes we hit the jackpot with their gifts.

Creating a family tradition is one of the most meaningful presents you can give. Our tradition was inspired by our son, Justin, when he was four. He was worried about the children who might not get a toy during the holiday season, so we started a project called the Miracle Maker campaign, which involves giving a toy to someone less fortunate than oneself. His entire school and others have adopted the project, and to date over ten thousand toys have been donated. The best gift of all continues to be brightening others' lives through kindness.

As you search through this chapter for the perfect presents to exchange with your family or friends during Hanukkah, consider a gift that will be meaningful and remembered long past the eight nights. Here are some suggestions that will brighten the nights of Hanukkah for someone you care about!

CHOCOLATE DREIDELS. Here's a present and an art activity all in one that will keep the kids occupied and happy. Teach them how to make their own Hershey's Kiss dreidels. Insert a toothpick into the base of an upside-down Hershey's Kiss, and instantly you'll have a spinning top that resembles a dreidel. Avoid using this with young children unless they are supervised, since the toothpicks have a sharp point. Teach the kids how to spin the dreidel, and then remove the toothpicks and gobble them up for a great gift that will be enjoyable and delicious, too.

DREIDEL, DREIDEL, DREIDEL. Start a dreidel collection and give a different dreidel every night of Hanukkah. Dreidels come in all shapes and sizes, from plastic to porcelain—and everything in between. Visit the local synagogue gift shop and you're bound to find a spectacular selection. Or, commission a local artist who works in clay, wood, or even glass to create one just for you.

BLACK HOUND NEW YORK. Call 1-800-344-4417 and request a catalog from one of New York's award-winning bakeries, dedicated to the art and craft of baking and chocolate making. They use only premium-quality natural ingredients, and their chocolates are delicious. You'll also love sending their assorted butter cookies, their chocolate pyramid, and other special-occasion cakes. All of their baked goods are handmade the old-fashioned way, with over four hundred different products available.

THE EIGHT NIGHTS OF HANUKKAH. Here's a wonderful tradition to make gift giving special during Hanukkah: a special theme is assigned to each night and gifts are exchanged with that theme in mind. From book night to game night to T-shirt night, you can cover all gift possibilities! One night could even be a mystery night with a surprise twist, but the idea here is to make gift giving fun and inventive.

THE SMARTEST COOKIE I KNOW. A gift I'll always treasure was the day my grandma, Annie Freedman, taught me how to bake her memorable chocolate chip cookies. Not only did she share with me her time-tested recipe, she also shared a lesson of love, filled with keen attention to every detail for creating perfect chocolate chip cookies. She gave me the precious gift of a family-honored tradition: Grandma Freedman's Cookies! (P.S.: While Grandma added a special ingredient—love—her recipe can be found right on the back of the Nestlé Toll House chocolate morsel bag!)

SYNAGOGUE GIFT SHOPS. The perfect resource for gifts for Hanukkah and other Jewish holidays is the gift shop at a local synagogue. Most synagogues have fabulous gift shops from which proceeds go to the synagogue and that feature a wide assortment of religious gifts. Consider giving a gift certificate from the synagogue so recipients can choose their own gifts. Or, check out sterling silver kiddush cups, challah covers, or Shabbat candleholders and give a gift that will be treasured and handed down through generations.

CHALLAH COVER. I've adored the challah covers my children have made for me over the years. A challah cover is a wonderful gift, especially when it's designed by a child. To make one, take a white cloth napkin and wash it to remove the sizing. Then encourage your child to use colorful permanent fabric markers to design a special challah cover that will be appreciated for years to come. Follow the directions on the fabric markers, and be sure to choose nontoxic ones. Wrap it around a loaf of challah bread and make a Friday night Shabbat absolutely perfect during the Festival of Lights.

FAMILY FUN. Put together the perfect family present by filling a basket with great gifts the entire family can use together: gift certificates for the movies, videotape rentals, the bowling alley, family-style restaurants, or even a game the entire family can play. This gift includes everyone in the fun and will definitely be appreciated by all.

A TISKET, A TASKET . . . HOW ABOUT A FRUIT BASKET? Call 1-800-237-3920 and request a catalog from Blue Heron. Since 1946, Blue Heron Gift Fruit Shippers has shipped Florida's finest, juiciest citrus fruit all over the country. From Indian River oranges and grapefruits to jumbo avocados, mangos, and organic apples, you'll find a fabulous assortment of the freshest gifts available. Be sure to check out their vine-ripened tomatoes (available during even the coldest weather), coconut patties, tropical marmalades, and their assorted tins packed with delicious treats and goodies. And don't forget to be creative with your greetings! When sending oranges add a note that says, "Orange you glad we're related (we're friends, etc.)?"

MAKE A MATCH. There's a magazine for everyone on your gift list. From fly-fishing to interior design, or whatever their interests, there's a magazine devoted to their favorite topics. For a wonderful gift, you could wish someone a happy, healthy Hanukkah and send a magazine that focuses on healthy living. Or, how about a gift subscription to the Jewish newspaper in their city? If you aren't sure which magazine to give, inquire at your favorite magazine stand and investigate the lineup of magazines.

HAPPY HERMAN'S. Call 1-800-825-6263 and order a free gourmet gift guide filled with a spectacular selection of gourmet gift baskets wrapped to perfection. Kosher products are also available for special-order baskets, so be sure to ask. An edible gift from Happy Herman's will keep everybody on your gift list happy.

DELI DELICACIES. Call 1-800-NYC-DELI and order a catalog from New York's Second Avenue Kosher Deli, one of the most well-known mail-order delicatessens. Give the gift of noshing and send a delectable two-pound kosher salami anywhere in the United States. Or, check out their divine deli delicacies, from rugalach to pickles to bagels and lox. Their products are outstanding and a real treat for anyone on your holiday list.

MUSIC TO YOUR EARS. Check out your local music stores for Judaica music for kids by Craig 'n' Company, one of our very favorite musicians. Purchase his CDs and cassettes: *My Jewish Discovery* and *My Newish Jewish Discovery*. You will also love Paul Zim's recordings, including *Zimmy Zim's Zoo and Noah's Ark, Too!* Both are available in many bookstores or can be found by calling 1-800-552-4088.

PICTURE PERFECT. This year at your Hanukkah party, why not make your gift the arrival of a professional photographer? Schedule one to come to the party and take group shots. Every year is so precious, and these photographs will always be reminders of happy times you've shared.

MENORAH MAGIC. Consider selecting a new menorah (the candelabra used during the eight nights of Hanukkah) for a special family on your Hanukkah list. You'll find a wide variety of menorahs in all shapes and sizes, from traditional to modern themes. Include a few packages of dripless candles for a special added touch. This is one gift that will definitely brighten things up!

A LOVE OF LEARNING. Want to give a gift that keeps on giving? Select a class or series of classes that teaches someone a new skill or enhances their knowledge of a particular topic. Check out the resources available in their neighborhood or at their synagogue for kosher cooking classes, Hebrew lessons, or other possibilities that just might be the best gifts of all.

CHOCOLATE EMPORIUM. Order a Hanukkah basket filled with chocolates, pretzels, popcorn, or the nosh of your choice from this kosher company that specializes in scrumptious hand-dipped gourmet chocolates. Inquire about their gourmet munchies and personalized chocolates, including pretzel sticks and chocolate kisses with your name or greeting on each. Call 1-888-CHOCLAT or visit their Web site at www.choclat.com.

KOSHER CORNUCOPIA. Call 1-800-7KOSHER (or go on-line at www.koshercornucopia.com) and talk to the gift experts at Kosher Cornucopia, a company dedicated to award-winning kosher specialty foods and gifts. You'll love their chocolate menorah treasure box filled with chocolate gelt, as well as the "magic tea chest," which is a wooden gift box containing an assortment of imported Israeli teas in a variety of flavors. Another sure winner is their delicious smoked salmon, which is wonderful on a bagel. Also be sure to check out their chocolate greeting cards that say "Happy Hanukkah." And just in case you aren't sure what to send, order one of their thematic gift baskets, perfect for all occasions. They'll even ship as far away as Israel.

NEED A HANUKKAH GIFT CONSULTANT? Call 1-305-661-3032 and speak to the gift consultants at Present Perfect, a gift store and basket company that specializes in unique Judaica gifts. Tell their gift experts what you need and they will recommend a present that is perfect for anyone on your gift list during Hanukkah or year round. While you're on the phone, inquire about their custom-made Bar and Bat Mitzvah gifts! Complimentary gift wrap is included on any gift.

THE SOURCE FOR EVERYTHING JEWISH. Call 1-800-426-2567 and order the most comprehensive catalog available for Judaica gifts. Hamaker Judaica, Inc., presents a spectacular catalog called the Source for Everything Jewish. It's America's largest and most diverse collection of mail-order Jewish gifts. Ritual and ceremonial objects, kosher gourmet gifts, fine art, books, audio and video, computer software, you name it! This catalog is jam-packed with great presents for Hanukkah, including magnificent menorahs, beautiful Stars of David, Limoges hinged porcelain dreidels, art, candlesticks, and much more. You'll find something for everyone on your Hanukkah gift list or for any holiday all year long.

Friendship Presents 7

*M*y dear friend Patty once wrote me that friends are the family we choose for ourselves. And how true! The gift of friendship is the perfect present in itself. Yet don't lose sight of the fact that expressing how you feel to a friend means so much. From being there in times of trouble to celebrating accomplishments and happy times, friends share the good and the bad. Letting someone know you're crazy about them means so much, and you're bound to make their day with your thoughtfulness.

When selecting a gift, consider what your friends love. Or, when offering a kind deed, think of things they don't like to do—cooking, for instance! Whatever their likes and dislikes are, match a present to their needs. Give a gift they really want. And of course, when in doubt, find out! Go back to my Perfect Present Survey (page 2) and ask your friend what she needs or what you might help with.

Friends are the jewels in life that require continuous care. Consider them precious: their presence is your perfect present.

GIVE AN IOU. If you have a friend who could use one more hour in the day or an extra pair of hands, give an IOU and create a coupon redeemable for driving a carpool, going grocery shopping, cooking your famous lasagna, or helping your friend get organized. The gift of your time or talent will definitely be appreciated as a true act of friendship when she needs a little help.

A RECIPE FOR FRIENDSHIP. The next time you discover a recipe for the perfect dinner or even a meal to make in minutes, make a copy and send it to a friend. From simple, easy-to-prepare meals for your busiest friend to gourmet dishes for your friend who loves to cook, there's a recipe that will stir up a smile on every friend's face.

 A GIFT THAT KEEPS GIVING. Perhaps you and a friend share a special interest, such as music, art, or history. Why not give that friend a membership in the local symphony, public radio station, performing arts group, museum, or other organization that supports the kinds of activities you two enjoy together? Let your friend know the gift is meant to express this thought: "I always feel like I belong when I'm with you."

PIECED WITH LOVE. Years ago, a friendship quilt was a traditional gift for a friend who was moving away. Each woman who was remaining behind would make a special quilt block, often including a personal sentiment for the soon-to-be-gone friend. All the blocks would then be assembled into a precious, one-of-a-kind coverlet. But don't wait until a friend plans to move; consider buying a quilt, making your own, or purchasing a pillow or smaller accessory that has been quilted, and express your friendship sentiments in a card saying, "You'll always be an important piece of my life!"

HAVE A FRIEND YOU LOVE TO SEA? Perhaps you feel like a fish out of water without a special friend nearby. Go overboard and let him know by calling 1-800-343-5804 and ordering a gift from the Legal Sea Foods® catalog. Legal Sea Foods serves or sells almost one hundred tons of fresh seafood every week in their restaurants, markets, and overnight mail-order business. From a complete lobster dinner to delicious smoked salmon or their famous clam chowder (which has even been served at presidential inaugurals), your seafood gift selection will be air-freighted overnight to your friend. (Or you can give a certificate so he can choose his favorite catch and the date it arrives at his shore!)

ACROSS THE MILES. Let your friend know you are always happy to hear from her by sending a prepaid long-distance phone card she can use anywhere, anytime, so she can talk to you for as long as she wants without worrying about the bill.

THINK THE WORLD OF SOMEONE? Express to your friend how important he or she is to your life. Send a globe or atlas with a note that says, "To the best friend in the whole wide world," or, "You mean the world to me." And if you want to take it one step further, plan a trip together or coordinate family vacations.

MAKE A DATE. Do you have a circle of friends who like to share important occasions such as birthdays and anniversaries? One meaningful gift would be a lovely calendar (chosen to reflect some special interest of your friend, be it gardening or golf), where you have gone through and marked the appropriate blocks with notations such as "Ali's birthday" and "Doug and Genie's anniversary" and highlighted all the important events your friend will want to note through the year. You could even add photographs each month to personalize the calendar. Accompany your calendar with an updated address book for an even more perfect gift.

OPPOSITES ATTRACT. Have you looked at salt and pepper shakers recently? They've become humorous collectibles in a wide range of styles and designs. If you think salt and pepper shakers are identical except for an S or P, look again. You can find a set where one is an oven, the other a chef; where one is a rabbit, the other a head of lettuce; where one is a fireman, the other a Dalmatian. Select an appropriate set and present it to your friend with a note that says, "We're two of a kind!"

GET ORGANIZED. Give your friend the gift of organization in case her life is too hectic all the time. From organizing an address book filled with her friends' addresses and special days to helping her control the paper in her house, she'll think you're Merlin the magician when you come to her rescue!

THE GIFT OF GAB. If your friend has been too busy or has been besieged by life, give him a call and an update of everything that's going on with your group of friends. Make sure he remembers special days, holidays, and occurrences in other friends' lives. Talk about great gifts; you'll make him look thoughtful, and he'll think you're absolutely the best friend ever!

FOR A SOUPER FRIEND. Pack up a basket of soups for a favorite friend and include a note saying, "A gift for my souper friend!" Or, call 1-800-253-0550 and order the Frontier Soups catalog, which is filled with fabulous ready-to-cook soup mixes that need only a few extra ingredients and can serve up to eight people. They'll package them up in a gift box and send them to your friend, who will think you're pretty super for being so thoughtful. Be sure to also check out their soups that are named for each state, such as Idaho Outpost Potato Leek, Connecticut Cottage Chicken Noodle, Carolina Springtime Asparagus Almond, and Texas Wrangler Black Bean. There's definitely a soup for everyone's taste!

SWEAT THE SMALL STUFF TOGETHER. Many people have a special friend who is a workout buddy. It might be someone who pushes you to improve your tennis game, makes sure you jog three miles a day, or grimaces with you during aerobics classes. A great gift would be a pair of athletic shoes along with a note that reads, "For the friend who keeps me on track." Or, if you know your friend needs a little encouragement in exercising, offer to go to the gym together or go on a weekly walk!

MAP IT OUT. City dwellers will probably appreciate this gift more than small-town folks. Give your friend a new, up-to-date map book showing every road, subdivision, office park, and shopping center in your area. Your note could read, "I'd be lost without you as a friend."

FOR A SCENT-SITIVE FRIEND. There are dozens of fabulous incenses and scented candles on the market. From cinnamon buns to chocolate chip cookies, you'll find a huge variety of scents. When your friend lights these candles they'll fill the air with the aroma of friendship.

HAVE A NEED TO MEND A FRIENDSHIP? Fill a basket with sewing items and express your feelings in case you have a friendship that needs mending. Add a note with your gift that says, "I hope we can mend things!"

HAVE A FRIEND WHO'S A SUPER SHOPPER? Your friend will thank you forever for one of the best catalog resources available. She'll discover more than 350 catalogs in seventy product categories in the Direct Marketing Association's latest edition of the *Great Catalog Guide*. Send your name and address with a $3.00 check or money order to: *Great Catalog Guide*, Consumer Services Dept., Direct Marketing Association, 1111 19th St. NW, Ste. 1100, Washington, D.C. 20036-3603.

GO TO ANY LENGTH. If your friendship is of immeasurable worth, give your friend a measuring tape. You could also give her measuring cups, spoons, and rulers to get your point across. Add a card that says, "I'd go to any length for you!" or, "Our friendship is immeasurable!" For an added touch, purchase an assortment of tape, from clear plastic tape to masking tape, and add a note that says, "Let's always stick together!"

MY FAVORITE THINGS. From fabulous places to shop for bargains to your favorite brand of nylon stockings or a particular hair spray that really works, pack up a colorful bag filled with your favorite things. Create a goodie bag for your favorite friend and share your latest and greatest finds, tips, and helpful advice.

PAPER PLUS! Personalized stationery is always a fabulous gift, especially if you have the envelopes imprinted with your friend's return address. You could also order some personalized note pads and gift enclosure cards. Fill a bag or basket with this creative assortment of stationery and paper, and get ready for the thank-you note of the century!

KNOW A GOOD SPORT? Perhaps you have a special friend with whom you've had a ball over the years. From tennis balls to golf balls, pack up the number of balls per years you two have played together. This gift is also great for friends' birthdays, anniversaries, or even to celebrate your years of employment together.

JUST ASK! Most friends will tell you exactly what they like, so be sure to ask. You'll generally get an earful of ideas, from favorite recording artists, authors, or restaurants to specific brands of clothing or accessories. Match up a gift certificate suitable for one of those items and give a present your friend will really love.

Congratulations Presents

*T*here are many occasions when congratulations are in order: a new job, a promotion, a long-anticipated accomplishment. Whatever the situation, it means so much to others to recognize and to share in their happiness.

The following gifts help celebrate the moment with your acknowledgment and feelings. Celebrate all sorts of special days, from pay raises to giving up smoking to cancer-free anniversaries. Sharing in someone else's achievements and milestones is a special opportunity to let them know how much you care. While you might never really know how meaningful your gifts of congratulations are, the joy of giving will be your greatest reward. You'll make someone else feel great and let him or her know that you noticed!

TO THE SWEET SMELL OF SUCCESS. From cakes to candy, send anything sweet to express your feelings, and add a note that says, "To the sweet smell of your success." In case someone you know is a chip off the old block or a smart cookie, call 1-800-COOKIES to request a catalog or place an order from Mrs. Fields, which has a fantastic selection of delicious cookies and gourmet gifts. You can also visit their web site at www.mrsfields.com.

 MOVING ON UP. If someone has accomplished something special and is on the rise, give a piece of luggage with personalized travel tags. Your note should read, "Congratulations, I hear you're going places!"

YOU'RE FLYING HIGH NOW. After years of being considered a children's toy, kites have come into their own, both as amusements for adults and as beautiful decorative objects. While cheap kites are available at discount stores, striking ones are available from a number of outlets. One catalog that specializes in kites is Into the Wind, at 1-800-541-0314. Once you've selected the perfect kite, present it with a note that reads, "Congratulations—we're certain you'll reach great heights."

OUTSTANDING IN YOUR FIELD. Send an attractive potted plant—choose something a little unusual, such as a colorful hibiscus in bloom or a bonsai—along with a note that says, "Congratulations. We're rooting for you!"

PUT SOME WEIGHT IN IT. Select a paperweight that you feel is appropriate—you'll find a whole range, from inexpensive ones in souvenir shops to beautiful crystal, silver, or collectibles available at jewelers and fine gift shops. Give the paperweight with a note that reads, "Congratulations. This is for the weighty decisions you'll be making." Or, if someone you care about has been waiting for test scores or a special acceptance letter, send a paperweight with a note reading, "Congratulations! Some papers are worth weighting for!"

WHAT A RISING STAR. Give a pair of sunglasses along with a note proclaiming, "Here's to your bright future." Or, fill a bag or basket with star-related items like star stickers, chocolate stars, or anything that has a star on it. Add a note that says, "When it comes to stars, you're shining bright!"

HATS OFF TO YOU. Many people, especially men, enjoy hats. Choose a baseball hat, wool golf cap, or straw hat and present it with a card reading, "Hats off to you!"

CRÈME DE LA CRÈME. Present your congratulations with a strawberry shortcake, covered with lots of real whipped cream. Your note should read, "The cream always rises to the top. You take the cake."

A BIG SUCCESS. Search for a stuffed-toy whale, mug, T-shirt, or anything that has a whale on it and present it with a note that says, "Congratulations on a whale of an accomplishment."

A MUG OF GOOD CHEER. Wish someone well on their accomplishment by filling a personalized or theme-related mug with hard candy, flavored coffee, or chocolates. Add a note that says, "Your cup runneth over, and we are filled to the brim with excitement for you!"

SWEETEN THE MOMENT. That's right! Go ahead and call 1-800-440-2131, and order someone special a congratulations basket from Giftcorp, a gourmet gift basket company I adore. Be sure to request their catalog and check out over twenty theme baskets that are filled to the brim with a variety of sweets, goodies, and delicacies. You'll also love sending their gift boxes and colorful totes, which come in a wide variety of themes and are packed with gourmet products. Choose from a new house to a doctor's bag to a briefcase and ship (in case their ship came in); these boxes and totes are a fabulous way to creatively say, "Congratulations!" You can also check their Web site at www.giftsbygiftcorp.com.

CHEER THEM ON TO VICTORY. Here's a gift that will definitely let someone know you are on their team. From a toy store, purchase cheerleader pom-poms and send them to someone whom you're proud to cheer on!

FROM YOUR BIGGEST FAN. Want a gift that will air your feelings? Select a desk-sized fan and include a note that says, "Congratulations from your biggest fan! Your accomplishment is really cool!"

HERE'S LOOKING AT YOU, KID! Give a mirror to someone who has impressed you with a special achievement. Add a note that says, "Mirror, mirror, please do show . . . the greatest kid we could ever know! P.S.: Look in this gift to see our choice!"

TO WHOM IT MAY CONCERN. Surprise a graduate or person you wish to encourage or congratulate with a letter of recommendation addressed "To whom it may concern," expressing your words of praise. Rave about the person's character traits and special achievements, and recommend them for any job they may pursue along their career path. Enclose a note that says, "It would be my privilege to recommend you in the near or far future. I hope this letter will come in handy one day. Feel free to use me as a reference for life!"

A CORNY GIFT. If someone you care about is popping at the seams with good news, why not give a corny gift? Fill a basket with a variety of popcorn products they'll be certain to enjoy.

THERE'S MUFFIN LIKE YOU! Rise to the occasion and send a gift from Wolferman's Fine Breads. Call 1-800-999-0169 and order a catalog from Wolferman's that features gourmet gifts, including English muffins, scones, cinnamon rolls, sticky buns, sensational brownies, and desserts that are out of this world. Include a note that says, "We'll rise to the occasion any day to congratulate you!"

Graduation Presents 9

*G*raduation from high school or college, or from anything for that matter, is a huge accomplishment. From high school to med school, when you commemorate that achievement, it means a great deal to both the graduate and his or her family. Long after the tassels have been turned and the diplomas framed, graduation presents signify a special time in one's life. While there are many meaningful gifts that exchange hands at graduation time, practicality is the key, especially when a graduate is going away to college or getting a first apartment or job.

Consider what will really be useful for the graduate when selecting a gift. Think about the climate and city the graduate is going to be living in, or inquire about the dorm room and other specific details. Search for creative ideas that will make him or her feel at home.

The following gift ideas will assist you in expressing your happiness and hearty congratulations in a number of creative ways. With any of these gifts in hand, you'll deserve a degree in creative gift giving yourself. There are also a few gifts featured that are appropriate for the student who will be graduating in a year or two. It's never too early to prepare for the big day! So go for it and enjoy searching for the perfect present for each of the graduates on your list!

GRADUATION ANTICIPATION. If there's a junior or senior on your gift list, or even a graduate considering grad school, then there are probably a few critical tests lurking in their future. Help them prepare with Kaplan Educational Centers, one of the nation's premier education companies. Kaplan provides individuals with a full range of resources to achieve their educational and career goals. Call 1-800-KAP-ITEM and order their catalog of courses and books.

MY HOMETOWN. For the graduate who is leaving home, combine a copy of Simon and Garfunkel's song "My Little Town" with a subscription to a newspaper or magazine from their hometown. This is somewhat sentimental, but it's nonetheless a treat to be able to read all about folks and events back home. Add a note that says, "No matter where you roam, you'll always have a place back home."

DON'T LEAVE HOME WITHOUT IT. Give the graduate a photograph of his or her entire family. Search for a combination frame that has a clock attached, and while time flies you can remind them that there's still no place like home!

THE GREATEST GRAD ON EARTH. Call 1-800-945-2552 and order the What on Earth catalog for a collection of fun clothing and delightful diversions. You'll find a selection of items featuring your grad's favorite television shows, themed T-shirts, gifts for animal lovers, and other worldly cosmic gifts, including many humorous presents and gag gifts.

THE GIFT OF ORGANIZATION. Give the graduate on your gift list the gift of organization with a gift certificate to a store that specializes in organizational devices. Call 1-800-733-3532 and order the Container Store catalog, with pages of fabulous organizers perfect for the graduate going away to college. No dorm room is complete without this company's helpful array of space-saving gadgets and accessories. They've got your graduate's needs covered!

PHONE HOME. Phone cards are an ideal gift for the graduate. Purchase them at most grocery or drug stores and even at many post offices. Combine this gift with an address book for an added touch, and of course list your own telephone number, so you'll be sure to get a call.

GOING PLACES? For the graduate who's going places, you'll find a perfect match in the Mori Luggage & Gifts catalog, filled with world-class luggage and leather goods. From high-tech electronics to thoughtful gifts and necessities for a traveling grad, this catalog is a terrific source for gifts. Call 770-451-MORI (in Atlanta, Georgia) or 1-800-678-MORI for a catalog or to locate the store nearest you.

HOME SWEET HOME. If you have a graduate who is away from home, pack up some of his or her favorite goodies and send them. You'll be surprised at how many things can be safely shipped overnight on ice. Also, consider Halloween an ideal time to sweeten up your college student's dorm room. You're never too old to love trick-or-treat candy, so satisfy your favorite graduate's sweet tooth with some goodies from home.

ALL CHARGED UP! For the graduate who is going on to graduate school, consider a gift that's really helpful. Since most graduates have a dozen or more electronic devices, fill up a box with assorted batteries for every occasion, and add a note that says, "We're proud that you've kept going and going and going!"

BACK TO THE BASICS. It's the little things that count, so give a gift that will be put to use. Graduates need just about everything, and would love a box or gift bag filled with some of the essentials. From stamps to note pads to pens, scissors, tape, and paper clips, make a bare-essentials kit for those little details.

CLIMBING THE LADDER. For a creative gift with a sense of humor, give a stepladder or a gift certificate for a favorite shoe store to the graduate on the rise. Add a note that says, "As you climb the ladder, we'll be watching your every step. Congratulations!"

INITIALLY YOURS. From personalized leather-bound dictionaries to portfolios, memo pads, and organizers, anything useful with a graduate's initials is a distinctive gift that will long be remembered.

PLEASE LEAVE A MESSAGE. An answering machine is a dorm room basic for the phone fanatic who doesn't want to miss a message. They come in all shapes and sizes, and your busy graduate will really put this one to use!

HERE'S A BULLETIN! Give your graduate a bulletin board and accessories such as push pins and photographs of friends and family for the dorm room. Not only will you dress up the room with familiar faces, but this gift will really be useful.

IF MOM CALLS . . . TELL HER TO SEND MONEY! Erasable message boards are another gift that is great for the graduate on the go. Not only are they useful, but they're reusable for years to come.

CITY SCENES. Give the graduate a poster or framed print of their city's skyline or a special scene of their hometown. Not only will it make them feel at home, but it will also add a scenic view to their otherwise gray dorm room.

TOTAL BED REST. Transform your graduate's bed into a comfort zone. Choose a totally comfortable corduroy bed rest for late-night studying. If you purchase one that has a removable cover for cleaning, you could have it personalized with the graduate's name or initials for a special touch.

THEY'LL LAP IT UP! They'll love a lap throw, afghan, or smaller blanket to cuddle up with in their dorm room. You'll find blankets from fleece to flannel in designs from school colors to plaids and solids. Every graduate will say thank you for this cozy, comfortable gift.

COMPUTE THIS! Computer accessories are great for the graduate who is a computer buff. From personalized or playful mouse pads to screen savers with the school logo and scenes from favorite sitcoms, you'll find a fabulous assortment of computer items the graduate will instantly put to use.

WORDS OF ADVICE. If you can't resist offering just a few little final instructions, give the graduate copies of the *New York Times* best-seller *Life's Little Instruction Book,* volumes 1 to 3, by H. Jackson Brown, Jr. (Rutledge Hill Press, 1991–1995). Over twenty million readers worldwide have celebrated these little plaid books, which offer inspirational suggestions, observations, and reminders on how to live a happy and rewarding life. Feel free to add a few of your own instructions at the end of the book to personalize your perfect present!

A DOSE OF INSPIRATION. *Chicken Soup for the Teenage Soul: 101 Stories of Life, Love, and Learning* by Jack Canfield, Mark Victor Hansen, and Kimberly Kirberger (Health Communications, 1997), is filled with touching stories that will inspire the graduate on your list. They'll eat up every serving of the words of wisdom in this meaningful book.

Mother's Day Presents

10

*M*other's Day is a special day that lets a mom know how much she is loved. Mother's Day comes once a year; however, most moms would prefer that every day be Mother's Day. Searching for a gift that a mom will love can be easy or difficult. Your mother, grandmother, aunt, or wife might love everything in sight, or might be someone who is very particular when it comes to gifts.

Choosing gifts for moms takes investigating weeks ahead of time. So don't wait until May to see what your mom might love. Begin your treasure hunt early. Watch your mom at stores as she admires things. Observe the kinds of things she's interested in. And don't forget that the best Mother's Day gifts have always been poems, letters expressing your love, children's art, and the thoughtfulness that goes into selecting or creating a gift.

When considering what your mom or spouse might want for Mother's Day, don't forget she's there for the asking. Most moms will tell you if they want to be surprised. Or, if she has her eye on a special piece of jewelry or particular present, she may let you know immediately. Ask for hints. Don't wait for the big day to almost arrive and then ask her what she wants.

The following gift ideas will help you as you search for the perfect present for your mom or a mom you love. Consider that MOM stands for "Make Ours Meaningful" and you'll never go wrong!

A PERFECT DAY. That's what my husband and children gave me for one Mother's Day, and it continues to be my all-time favorite gift. The best part was that I got to define exactly what a perfect day meant. Believe it or not, my perfect day included having the garage finally cleaned out, the grocery shopping done, everyone getting along beautifully, eating out . . . my every desire! It was the best Mother's Day gift ever, and my every whim was met with enthusiasm and smiling faces. What more could a mom ask for?

GOOD NIGHT, MOM. Whoever said "nighttime was made for parents" must have known what it was like to be a mom. Celebrate how hard Mom works all day by giving her a good-night gift! Fill a basket with nighttime presents including a nightgown, relaxing music, and a favorite author's latest book for late-night reading when she can't fall asleep. Add a card that says, "Here's a good-night gift because we love you. Thank you for everything you do all day long!"

A SCENT-SATIONAL GIFT. If your mom loves scents, tell her she's scent-sational with the gift of perfume. Select a scent that reminds you of her or choose one of her all-time favorites, perhaps even a scent she wore as a young girl. Wrap up your gift with a card that tells her all the reasons she's so sensational!

FOR KITCHEN LOVERS ONLY. If your mom is a kitchen enthusiast, she'll love the Sur la Table catalog. Call 1-800-243-0852 for a complimentary catalog filled with a magnificent collection of top-quality domestic and professional kitchen equipment, including gadgets, knives, books, molds, small appliances, and linens. Unusual and hard-to-find items are available through worldwide contacts, and they offer something for everyone who loves to cook. Order the catalog early so Mom can put a star by her favorite items. Perfect words to add with creative molds in the shapes of hearts and angels are, "They broke the mold when they made our mom!"

KEEP MOM CURRENT! Call 1-800-643-0042 and order Current, Inc., a free catalog filled with sensational stationery and cards in appealing designs, in a variety of motifs. Mom will love their personalized stationery, all-occasion and holiday cards, gift wrap, organizers, and much more. Stock up Mom with an assortment of their products and she'll be ready to write on a moment's notice!

TIME OUT. Give Mom time off from all the chores that come with her position. Cook dinner for an entire weekend, unload the dishwasher, do the laundry. That's right! Mom gets a weekend off. Long baths, feet up, totally indulged. Pamper her, adore her, wait on her, but make sure she's totally given time off! Talk about a perfect present . . . that's it!

PROMISES, PROMISES. Give Mom peace of mind by writing down all the promises you feel comfortable making to her. From never drinking and driving to always locking your car door, be creative and make a meaningful list. P.S.: Don't forget to promise to love her forever and ever, even if she serves leftovers.

UNTIL THE END OF TIME. Give Mom a gift she'll adore through time. Buy her a crystal or silver clock and add a note that says you'll treasure her "until the end of time."

TAKE NOTE. You can make your own stationery and greeting cards for Mom to use all year long by taking a drawing to a copy store and having it duplicated on card stock. They can reduce your image and make fold-over notes in a flash. Purchase envelopes ahead of time and match them up for a professional set of stationery she'll treasure.

MOM'S NUMBER ONE. For the mom who's number one on your list, create a special tradition in her honor and give her a dozen Mother's Days! Make the first day of each month your Mom's Day. Do special things like taking out the trash, filling a vase with flowers, or writing her a special note of appreciation. She'll think you're number one for thinking of her in such a creative way.

GOT A BLUE-JEANS MAMA? If your mom is totally cool and loves wearing jeans, or if you want your mom to kick off her high heels and relax a bit, call 1-800-USA-LEVI. Levi Strauss & Co. is the world's largest apparel manufacturer, and thanks to Levi's® custom-fitting jeans program, you can indulge Mom in perfect-fitting jeans. Levi Strauss & Co. offers Original Spin jeans in their Original Levi's Stores™, so inquire about the location nearest you. These jeans are personalized to a woman's body using a special computer program to assist with the fit and measurement. Consider a gift certificate, or take Mom out for a surprise shopping spree. Make the "ultimate fit" your perfect present! (Orders cannot be accepted by telephone or mail.)

DON'T LET IT RAIN ON MOM'S PARADE! It might sound like a simple gift, but I promise Mom will love it. Purchase a few small, colorful fold-up umbrellas. Test one first and make sure you love it, and then purchase one or be bold and buy a different color and pattern for every day of the week. Add a note that says, "I hope it never rains on your parade!" or, "No raindrops on my mom's head. You're way too special!"

HAVE A PEARL OF A MOM? If your mom is a real jewel, but your budget can't handle the real thing, call 1-800-797-5378 and request the Erwin Pearl catalog, which features a magnificent collection of costume jewelry that looks authentic. Ask about their White House Collection, inspired by the Camelot legend. With his Fifth Avenue store, Erwin Pearl re-created the thrill of walking into a big candy store by offering thousands of styles of beautiful jewelry, and you can't go wrong with his gifts.

IT'S THE LITTLE THINGS THAT COUNT. Looking for the perfect words to express your thoughts or ideas, stay connected, and strengthen the bonds between friends and family? Check out my book *When Words Matter Most: Thoughtful Deeds for Every Occasion* (Crown Publishers, 1996) and *Little Things Shared: Lasting Connections Between Family and Friends*, by Susan Newman, Ph.D. (Crown Publishers, 1998). Both books are filled with creative ideas that will inspire anyone on your gift list, especially Mom and Grandma.

NOTHING'S TOO GOOD FOR MOM. Call Borsheim's, America's largest independent jewelry store, at 1-800-642-GIFT, and order their magnificent complimentary annual catalog. Borsheim's features every imaginable gemstone set in silver, gold, and platinum to dazzle your mom or any special someone on your list. They also feature a wide selection of fine presents and collectibles. With over 127 years in business, they wrote the book on making their customers happy.

GIVE MOM A MASTERPIECE. Call 1-800-459-7215 and order one of the most precious gifts you'll ever give. Have artwork made into a one-of-a-kind handcrafted piece of jewelry in sterling silver or fourteen karat gold for Mom. KiDoodles are created by an artist named Joy Hannan-Copanezos who specializes in transforming children's drawings into wearable pins, necklaces, or earrings.

PLAN A GETAWAY. A surprise trip is the perfect present for the mom who needs a break, loves to travel, and doesn't have the time or energy to plan a trip. From a visit to a spa just for Mom or a quick trip to a nearby resort with the entire family, plan a mystery trip and give her miles of smiles!

CALLING ALL SHOPPERS. Call 1-800-345-4500 and order the Spiegel catalog, the lifestyle resource for the working woman. This catalog specializes in exclusive products, clothing, gifts, accessories, home furnishings, toys, and just about everything a person could wish for! It's jam-packed with wonderful ideas that change seasonally and provide one-stop shopping for a woman's entire wardrobe.

HAVE A FASHIONABLE MOM? For a wonderful resource filled with stylish clothing and unique items that Mom will adore, check out the J. Peterman Company Catalog by calling 1-800-231-7341. This is the company that brought you a chance to own movie props and replicas from the movie *Titanic*. You'll also find a unique selection of gifts and extraordinary items for the mom who appreciates fine things at an affordable price.

SHOP TILL YOU DROP! Call 1-800-285-5800 and request a complimentary catalog from Nordstrom, one of America's favorite catalog companies. Nordstrom features a marvelous selection of shoes, clothing, and accessories any mom will love. Order a copy and let Mom select her wish list without ever leaving home.

Father's Day Presents

 **S**ome dads are a real challenge when it comes to selecting gifts that they will love, while others are a total cinch. My dad, for example, is a big softie, but really hard to please when it comes to the perfect present. It's not because he doesn't adore and appreciate our efforts; he's just very particular. Finding something he really needs takes an enormous amount of thought, since he's the ultimate shopper and knows exactly what he likes and doesn't like. But year after year, we've gone to great lengths and the effort is always worth it. So let the shopping begin!

Over the years we've learned a lot from our dad about selecting the ideal gift. The secret in his case, and with many other dads, is to involve him in the process. We get the particulars, find out the type of luggage or shirt or tie he's been looking for. We make certain we listen to every detail, and then the hunt begins. Some years, though, we quickly vote on a gift certificate and let him do the deciding! But no matter what, his happiness is our main objective and we've become very good at succeeding.

As you search for a present for a father you adore, don't leave any stone unturned. The perfect present is waiting for you right around the corner!

HAVE A TRAVELIN' DAD? If your dad is frequently in the air or on the road, call Mori Luggage & Gifts at 1-800-678-MORI and order a fabulous catalog filled with a diverse selection of luggage, briefcases, travel accessories, leather goods, and much more. Check out Dad's traveling accessories and see what needs replacing. Or involve him in the selection of an item from the catalog. When giving it to him add a note that says, "No matter where you go, our love for you will always show."

A DOZEN FOR DAD. Okay, so your dad loves one particular type of pajama or sock or even undershirt. Give him a dozen pairs, one in every color, or stock up on the exact size and color he prefers to wear. Some dads like the same old thing, and your dad will appreciate having an ample supply on hand.

HAVE A DO-IT-YOURSELF DAD? Call 1-800-423-2567 and order the Harbor Freight Tools catalog, with thousands of quality brand-name tools for the do-it-yourselfer or the professional. Dad will love this 115-page catalog and its fabulous selection of tools for every project imaginable.

AS TIME GOES BY. Take a picture every year of all the children surrounding Dad. Have it enlarged and framed and give him a copy. As the years go by, these photographs will be one of his greatest treasures. At home or the office, he'll spend many a moment recalling all of the happy times you spent together.

TIED TO PERFECTION. Call 1-800-922-8437 and request a Ralph Marlin & Co., Inc., catalog filled with just about every tie imaginable. This company specializes in themed ties that will suit your dad to a T. Whether your father is hooked on sports or plays a certain instrument, you'll discover a colorful assortment of ties with designs from the Three Stooges to Dilbert to NFL and automotive ties. The catalog is also jam-packed with a variety of silk ties, polyester ties, T-shirts, boxers, caps, and more.

GIFTS GALORE. Call 1-800-543-3366 and order the Hammacher Schlemmer catalog to discover a world of gifts that are perfect for every dad. Offering the best-quality items, including fabulous accessories, specialty umbrellas, high-tech gadgets, monogrammed robes, car covers, and the unexpected for over 148 years, this company has hundreds of terrific gifts that will definitely please your dad.

FOR THE SWEETEST DAD ON EARTH. Perhaps your dad loves a certain kind of candy or has a sweet tooth for a particular type of cake. Stock up Dad's candy jars at the office or at home, or fill up the freezer with special sweet or frozen things he really adores. Add notes to each that say, "To the sweetest [or coolest] dad on Earth!"

TOOL TIME. Call 1-800-358-3096 and order a catalog from Tool Crib of the North, serving customers since 1948. This catalog is packed with the finest woodworking and construction tools in the world. Dad will love this catalog, and with this perfect present you might even get him to repair something just for you!

BOOKS ON TAPE. If your dad or a dad you know spends a lot of time in the car, purchase a selection of books on tape that he'll enjoy. Focus on his particular interest and give him a super selection of audio books. He'll love getting an earful of sound advice or listening to a great novel while on the road or stuck in traffic.

PICTURE THIS. Find a photograph of your father in his earlier days. Maybe he was a war veteran and dressed in his uniform, or perhaps there's a picture of him playing baseball, holding his favorite pet, or standing beside his first car. Have the photograph restored or enlarged and brought back to its prime with the help of a photography expert.

HAVE A HIGH-TECH DAD? If your dad has a fascination with high-tech gadgets, check out the Sharper Image catalog by calling 1-800-344-4444 for a fabulous selection of great presents, including the latest and greatest gadgets and accessories that every dad will appreciate. Whether Dad is a businessman, sportsman, or traveling dad on the go, you'll find something super here! Or, if you aren't sure what to get him, purchase a gift certificate from the Sharper Image and combine it with a catalog for at-home shopping. Any couch potato dad will enjoy this!

WHAT'S COOKING? Ask Dad what favorite dishes or meals his mom made when he was a little boy, and prepare them especially for him with love. From his favorite dessert to soups Mom made him when he was under the weather, do a little homework and get the scoop. If these dishes can be frozen, make a few extra for the freezer. If you aren't a whiz in the kitchen, consider hiring a caterer who can prepare these items. Talk about a thoughtful gift—this one will take a little work but will be appreciated more than you'll ever know.

TAILOR MADE. If your dad does not like to shop, find a shopping service or tailor who will arrive at his door and custom fit his every wardrobe need. From suits to slacks, provide a gift certificate so he can shop from his office or at his home.

Valentines and Other 12
Romantic Presents

*L*ittle expressions of love always go a long way and are a
meaningful way to let someone else know how you feel. While the
big gifts become memorable testimonies to one's affection, it's often
the little things that keep us connected and in tune with each other.

Romantic gifts come in all shapes and sizes, and the gift of your
feelings does not even cost a thing. My favorite example is a day
when my husband gave me a big hug and said, "Have I told you how
great you are lately?" Those words meant the world to me. Try saying it to someone you care about—you'll see how special it makes
them feel.

The following ideas are creative expressions of love. When we try
one, we also feel good about ourselves. By giving lov-
ing acts of kindness, we illustrate to others how we
enjoy being treated. So add some fun back into

your relationship. Spend an hour or even more conjuring up something that will make your mate's day. Not only will you cheer that special someone up, but you'll show that you really, really care.

MUSIC TO MY EARS. Choose a song that's played by your mate's favorite musician. From the Beatles' "I Want to Hold Your Hand" to Stevie Wonder's "You Are the Sunshine of My Life," purchase a song on CD or cassette and dedicate it to your sweetie. Surprise her by cueing up the tape in her car, so when she turns on the engine the song will play!

STRETCH YOUR POINT! One of the most romantic evenings I've had was the time my husband surprised me with an evening on the town. A stretch limousine arrived at the door, and we then picked up a close friend who had planned this surprise for his wife as well! Our husbands took us to dinner, made beautiful toasts, and gave us each a gift, for absolutely no reason at all. Talk about romantic—an evening of wining and dining with a limo for transportation definitely made a long-lasting memory.

WORDS OF LOVE. Words, wonderful words . . . they're free and fabulous and waiting for you to grab them and put them to use. So be creative. Is she reading a new book? Add a little love note inside. Is he working out on a regular basis? Include a note in his gym bag. From refrigerator notes to greeting cards, consider the presence of your thoughts the perfect way to say "I love you."

LOVE IS ALWAYS IN SEASON. If your partner's favorite food is something that is in season for only a short amount of time, freeze it, can it, or store it in some other way that allows you to create an out-of-season surprise. From raspberries to Girl Scout cookies, season your relationship with a gift that will make him smile and show you care.

A TREE-MENDOUS TOKEN OF YOUR AFFECTION. Go out on a limb and give your spouse a tree! Perhaps it's time to spruce up the landscaping or plant a few new trees. If so, plant a thought with them that proclaims your growing affection, and tie a ribbon around the tree with a card that says, "My love for you is tree-mendous!"

BRIGHTEN UP HIS DAY. Write "I love you" right on a lightbulb with a permanent marker, and replace the bulb in a household lamp or a desk lamp in his office. Not only will you brighten up his day, but you'll say "I love you" in bright lights. Talk about lighting up his life! He'll always remember this enlightening gift, and if there's not a lamp nearby, gift wrap the bulb and leave it on his desk.

FLOWER YOUR PARTNER WITH ATTENTION. Send a beautiful bouquet of flowers in bloom with a note that says, "Here's to a blossoming relationship—ours!"

PRINCE CHARMING TO THE RESCUE. Want to charm her for the rest of your life with a sentimental gift? For a special occasion, give her a charm bracelet with a charm to commemorate that event. For example, if it's her birthday, give her a charm bracelet with a birthday cake charm on it. Include a note that says, "You're the icing on the cake!" Next, add a heart on Valentine's Day with a note that says, "You have a heart of gold." Your local jeweler should have a catalog that features every imaginable charm, and many can be engraved with your initials together or even an "I love you"!

START AN "I LOVE YOU" TRADITION. Initiate a weekly ritual that you and your mate do, such as a night at the movie theater or trying out a new restaurant. You could also stay home, rent a movie, and have a popcorn night. Or, consider exchanging a greeting card every Friday expressing your feelings for each other. Whatever you do, stick to the plan as often as possible. You'll stay connected and make each other feel like a priority.

RENT A CAR. Here's a gift that will take you back in time. Rent a car from the past that takes you back to a special time in your lives. From a convertible to a GTO to a Mustang or the car of your mate's dreams, take your sweetie for a spin and paint the town red! While the exact model might be difficult to locate, if you do find it, just watch the mileage you get with this idea!

MIXED UP OR ACTING A LITTLE NUTTY? There's nothing like a good old apology to bring back the romance in your relationship. Give it a try. If you acted a little nutty and hurt the one you love, pick up a jar of mixed nuts and attach a note asking for their forgiveness. If you really want to smooth things over, make your apologies chocolate-covered. Who could resist this romantic gesture?

FOR A REAL PEARL. Give a timeless gift, a strand of pearls. Visit your local jeweler and get educated about these gifts from the sea. If you can't afford the real thing, consider ordering a beautiful copy. Call 1-800-797-5378 and order the Erwin Pearl catalog, which features a wonderful selection of fine fashion jewelry. Add a note that says, "When it comes to jewels, you're mine!"

WILD ABOUT SOMEONE? For a fun gift, give your mate a membership to your city's zoo and a note that says, "I'm wild about you!"

OCEANS OF LOVE. While at the beach, write "I love you" in the sand, add your mate's name, and take a picture of it. Frame the photo and give this expression of love, ready to stand the mightiest waves of time.

YOU'RE THE SPICE IN MY LIFE. Call 1-800-551-9066 and order a catalog from Creole Foods of Opelousas (Louisiana), which makes Tony Chachere's Famous Creole Seasoning and other Cajun/Creole cooking and seasoning products. Let your mate know how much his spiciness livens up your day.

SEND YOUR LOVE VIA WESTERN UNION. Take your mate by surprise and send the real thing—a telegram! Call 1-800-325-6000 and order a telegram, which will cost between $30.00 and $50.00 plus tax for one to fifteen words. It will be delivered within five hours depending on the time it is sent.

FREEZER PLEASERS. Fill your refrigerator or freezer with little "I love you" gifts. With a marking pen, write little sayings straight from your heart, like . . . on the olive jar, "Olive you!" Or, on the pickles, "Sorry if I was sour!" Or on the orange juice, jot, "Orange you glad we're married?" And don't forget the egg carton—write, "Humpty Dumpty sat on the wall and said 'I love *you* most of all!'"

MUSIC TO HER EARS. Display your love in public and give a gift your mate (and the entire restaurant where you give it) will never, ever forget. Hire a violinist to play a few love songs and serenade your sweetheart after dinner. Coordinate with the waiter to deliver a gift especially from you along with the dessert. From a heart of gold on a necklace to something else she's always wanted, choose a special gift and songs of love that will make this the most memorable present you've ever given.

SAY IT WITH CHOCOLATE. Godiva Chocolatier, the world's leading super-premium chocolate brand, produces more than two hundred different chocolate pieces that are often mixed and matched to create a wide range of collections ideal for gift giving. For someone with a heart of gold, give Godiva's classic box, the Gold Ballotin, or for the sweetest person on Earth, check out their famous truffles and magnificently molded pieces. Call 1-800-9-GODIVA to order products for delivery anywhere in the United States or to request a Godiva catalog featuring a comprehensive selection of year-round favorites and the latest seasonal collections. Cybershoppers can order products at the Godiva Online World Wide Web site at www.godiva.com or through America Online: keyword Godiva.

FOREVER KISSES. Wish someone special a happy Valentine's Day by filling up an enormous basket or huge glass or plastic container with Hershey's Kisses. Add a note that says, "Forever kisses just for you. Even though yours are sweeter, hope these will do!"

PUT YOUR HEART INTO IT! My dad did this for my mom one year. Purchase a box of Valentine's Day cards, which usually come twenty-four or more to a box. Sign each one or write little notes, put them in envelopes, and hide them in places around your house for your valentine to find. Nothing's off limits—from the refrigerator to her shoes, anything goes!

EATS FOR YOUR SWEETS. Delicious M&M's® candies can be put to use in a totally creative way. Purchase a large bag and sort out all the blue ones, and put them in a container. Add a note that says "I'm blue without you," or fill a jar with orange M&M's and include a card that reads, "Orange you glad I love you?"

IN CONCERT WITH EACH OTHER. Okay. Your mate's favorite musical group is coming to town and tickets are at a premium. So what? Don't waste any time—be the first in line to grab a pair. Surprise your partner with this monumental gesture of your affection. Add dinner for two for a perfect evening and a gift to be remembered forever and ever.

Grandparents' Presents

I adored my grandparents, and our children certainly adore theirs. Grandparents are so special, and there's a special place in their hearts for those gifts from their children, grandchildren, and some-times even great-grandchildren. From photographs to poems, the gifts that make grandparents happiest are the ones that are straight from the hearts of those they love.

The following ideas mix sentimental presents with those gifts that actually have a function. Most grandparents will appreciate things they can put to use. This chapter focuses on many practical items they will not only use, but reuse and value throughout the years. You'll also find many gifts that reflect the bare necessities of life. Sav-ing Grandma or Grandpa from running out for extra stamps or supplying them with a safety gadget or helpful service just might be the perfect present.

So look no further. Just check out these gifts and then think of one that will please that special grandparent in your life!

MATURE MART. Call 1-800-720-6278 (MART) and order the Mature Mart catalog, which features quality products for today's seniors. From kitchen utensils and cutlery that are easy to grip, easy-to-tie shoelaces, telephone amplifiers, jumbo-print playing cards, and even an alarm clock that vibrates for the hard of hearing, this company has a fabulous selection of perfect presents for Grandma and Grandpa alike! Gift baskets and gift certificates are also available.

A GRAND IDEA. Using a tape recorder, tape your family's feelings about why Grandma or Grandpa is so grand! You could begin your tape with, "How do we love you, Grandma. Let us count the ways," and then let each family member express a thought. This could go on for eternity, but fifteen minutes of grand thoughts for your special grandparent will surely make his or her day!

H_2O TO GO. Here's a gift that's no sweat! Check out your local home-delivery filtered or spring water options, and order a home system for a very cool grandparent. You could give a year's worth of H_2O or a gift certificate toward services. There are many water systems that fit in small areas of the kitchen, and various options are available. Or a water filtration system is a cost-efficient option.

DON'T ALARM THEM . . . but you can really give an important gift by giving the grandparents on your list a fire alarm or carbon monoxide detector. If they already have a fire alarm, be sure to check it out to see that it is properly working. Make sure they have a fire escape plan and know what to do in an emergency. They might have taught you all these things when you were growing up, but now it's time to return the favor and check in on them!

THIS IS YOUR LIFE. One of the greatest gifts I gave my grandmother, and then ultimately myself and our entire family, was the videotape on which I interviewed her about her life. Sounds simple, but I promise there will never be a greater gift than celebrating someone you love by getting their life story on tape. From where Grandma was born to special childhood memories to how she met Grandpa, she lovingly answered every question I asked and offered special comments about every family member. When my grandmother passed away, the tape became a gift to my entire family and one of the most precious possessions we'll ever have. Grandma's thoughts about how much she loved all of us were captured, and the tape will serve as a family treasure for generations to come.

BREATHE EASY. Or easier, that is, with a humidifier installed in their heating and air-conditioning system. Check out the available options from a reputable dealer and see if it's a gift that will improve their atmosphere. There are also humidifiers that are single units and fit on a bedroom counter, but be sure to check with your parent or your grandparent's physician to get their opinion on what is really needed.

THIS OLD HOUSE. Commission an artist to create a rendering of your grandparents' house, or if they've moved to an apartment, their last home. You could also take a photograph of the home as it looks today and have it mounted next to an earlier photo. Enclose a card or add an engraved plaque mounted on the frame that says, "Home sweet home is wherever you roam."

CLUTTER-FREE CLOSETS. As time moves on, closets seem to get smaller and smaller. Give your grandparents the luxury of organized closets. Hire a professional closet planner and have their closets improved. From hangers and shelves they can reach to extra storage devices, they'll be thrilled to have more space and less clutter.

TAPE UPDATE. Take your family's old movies and have them transferred to videotapes they can view at home. Some companies will put them to music and will also be able to use or include still photographs. Or, if your grandparents have a box of old photographs that have never been organized in a photo album, consider doing the job for them. Label who is who and create a family tree and place it in the front of the book. And last but not least, if your grandparents' wedding album is falling apart, have it restored or even transferred into a new wedding album imprinted with their names and wedding date.

IT'S A TRIP! This one's worth saving for! One of the most exciting presents you can ever give grandparents who have time on their hands and the ability to travel is a dream trip to a place they've never visited. From round-trip tickets to taking care of all of the details, plan the perfect trip and give a present that's out of this world. One word of advice: make sure the destination is the ideal match, and do your homework before confirming any details.

FREE FOR ALL. Everyone loves to get something for nothing, and there are many free services and special discounts for seniors in your community. Enlist the help of your entire family, and check out all the free goods and services available for your grandparents. While they might already know of quite a few things that are free, you're bound to uncover some new opportunities. From discounted travel to special discounts at a grocery store to a free cup of coffee, get the scoop on what's free around the neighborhood for super seniors.

PACK IT UP. Now that your grandparents have more time to travel, take them with you to a luggage store and let them choose matching luggage. Even if they can't agree, it's still their choice! Have brightly colored luggage tags personalized so no matter where they are, baggage claim is a breeze.

HOW ABOUT A NIGHT OUT? Good ol' gift certificates are still one of the best standbys on Earth. Your grandparents will love receiving them for their favorite restaurant, movie theater, video rental store, or you name it! So put together a basket of nights out for Grandma and Grandpa and watch the smiles on their faces.

THE BIGGER THE BETTER. Many magazines are available in a larger type size. Not having to squint or always put on glasses makes this the perfect present for Grandma or Grandpa. Call the 1-800 information directory at 1-800-555-1212 for a favorite magazine's subscription number or the customer service number and inquire about the availability of magazines in large type.

STAMPS PLUS. Here's a gift that will win a definite stamp of approval! Give your grandparents a big supply of self-sticking postage stamps. You could also include a letter opener, a magnifying glass, a collection of easy-grip pens, or any other stationery tools and accessories that will make their job easier. This is a useful gift they'll really appreciate. For additional information about stamps and ways you can purchase them from home, call the United States Postal Service at 1-800-STAMP-24 and order the Stamps Etc. catalog.

LARGER THAN LIFE. There are now telephones and other gadgets that have extra-large numbers. A telephone with jumbo numbers makes a wonderful gift for a grandparent who is vision-impaired or needs a little help. Check out your local telephone store or electronics store.

NOT JUST FOR THE BIRDS. My mother loves bird-watching, and one year we gave her a beautiful birdhouse and a book about birds. This is a relaxing pastime and really enjoyable! You could also include binoculars or birdseed or purchase a birdbath, too.

Forgive-Me Presents 14

*L*et's face it . . . we all mess up at one time or another. Even though we don't want to hurt someone's feelings, we often inadvertently do. This chapter is dedicated to a variety of ideas to help you beg for forgiveness in a creative way. While some situations require more than just a clever gesture, the premise of these gifts is that you care enough to take the time to show how sorry you really are. A gift of apology illustrates your feelings of remorse and lets the other person know his or her feelings are important to you.

The following gifts range from the silly to the genuinely heartfelt. Whatever you do, match the moment and don't underestimate the meaning or act of saying, "I'm sorry." It is not something you say repeatedly, for at some point it loses its meaning, especially if your actions don't support it. However, when apologies are heartfelt and sincere, perhaps they become the best gift of all.

LOST YOUR NOODLE? Call 1-800-566-0599 and order a catalog from the Flying Noodle. If you've been repeatedly late to dinner and want to apologize, send their Pasta Club, which delivers a different collection of gourmet pastas and sauces (enough for about ten dinners) to the recipient's doorstep every month. An Italian dinner for two? That just might take the sting out of a conflict. Be sure also to visit their Web site at www.flyingnoodle.com.

DID YOU MAKE THEM NUTS? Call 1-800-872-6879 and order the Hammons Pantry catalog. They will send a fabulous assortment of delicious nuts anywhere in the world. That's right . . . send assorted apologies and add a note with your sincerest plea for their forgiveness: "Sorry for driving you nuts."

HOT AND BOTHERED? If you simply bothered someone and want to apologize, give a bottle of Tabasco sauce with a note that says, "If you're not still hot and bothered, how about dinner soon? I promise to pour on the apologies. I'm sorry!"

PEAS FORGIVE ME. Here's an idea that is totally uncanny. On a can of peas, tape or write a message that says, "Peas forgive me!" You could also add a head of lettuce that says, "Lettuce make up. I promise to turn over a new leaf."

HEART OF HEARTS. Here's an apology for every budget. Give someone a heartfelt message. You could purchase a chocolate heart, glass heart, or heart of any substance and size, and add an apology and message straight from your heart.

MAKE SOMEONE GO BANANAS? Here's a fun play on words. If you drove someone totally bananas, purchase a bunch of bananas and write your apology on it with a permanent marker. Hopefully, you'll be out swinging soon!

WRITE NOW. Okay, so candy and flowers simply won't work. How about expressing your feelings of remorse in writing? That's right, sit right down and write a card or letter now! Consider the other person's feelings and address what occurred specifically. Don't just say you're sorry; say what you're sorry for.

ON THE MEND. Apologize by giving him a box of Band-Aids. Add a note that says, "I'm sorry I hurt your feelings. I hope we can be on the mend soon."

I'M SORRY I BLEW IT! Send a balloon bouquet with a note that says, "I'm sorry I blew it. Can I rise to the occasion with an apology? I won't let you down again."

A DAY OFF. The only way to make up for those unavailable hours when she really needed you is to give her the gift of time. Spend a day off with her and give her the opportunity to tell you everything she wants you to do. It's a great way to say "I'm sorry" and a meaningful way of making up for lost time!

GET THE POINT. So it took you a little while to get the message and see your way through the problem. Now that you're ready to apologize and tell her she was right, do so in a clever manner. Purchase a dozen pencils in all different colors, and tie them up with a bow. Add a note that says, "I got the point. You were write!"

A PENNY FOR YOUR THOUGHTS. Go to the bank and request one hundred shiny new pennies. Wrap them up in a box with a note that says, "I'm sorry, I just didn't use any cents! Forgive me!"

YOU TAKE THE CAKE. Wrap up an angel food cake in colorful plastic wrap and add a note that says, "I promise to be a total angel. I hope you'll forgive me."

ON THE RECORD. Give a musical apology that will play on and on. Consider the Beatles' "With a Little Help from My Friends." Choose a record with songs on it that sum up your feelings, and add a note that says, "Just for the record, it was totally my fault."

POP RIGHT IN! Pop right in with an apology. Pop a big bowl of popcorn and offer it as a peace offering. He might think it's a corny idea, but you'll both probably enjoy it just the same.

BEAN ROTTEN LATELY? Round up the jelly beans and fill a jar. Add a note that says, "I'm sorry I've bean so difficult lately. I hope you'll accept my apology."

ETCH YOUR APOLOGY IN STONE. It'd be wonderful if that was readily possible, but the next best thing to etching your apology in stone is to write it on an Etch-A-Sketch. Purchase this time-tested toy at your local toy store, and then spend your time figuring out how to etch the words "I'm sorry!" If you're really confident of your Etch-A-Sketch skills, feel free to even add a few hearts! Your efforts will certainly be noticed, but if you still feel you must etch it on stone, your best bet is to use sidewalk chalk.

BEEN A LITTLE CRABBY LATELY? Here's a fun way to make up in case you've been a little moody lately. Plan a special dinner and order stone crabs from one of the country's most famous restaurants—Joe's Stone Crab, open for over eighty-five years. Call 1-800-780-CRAB (2722), order a brochure, and talk to Florida's stone-crab experts. They will send your fully cooked stone-crab dinner, complete with instructions on cracking the claws!

Get-Well Presents and Expressions of Sorrow

When someone you care about is ill or not feeling well, there are endless gifts that will cheer them up and express your feelings. Sometimes a greeting card or donation to a good cause is appropriate, while other times a gift that the person can really enjoy while recuperating is best. Consider how long your friend or loved one will be under the weather and match the gift accordingly. Is he confined to bed? Does she have a lot of time to fill and enjoy reading? Or, would meals for her family in disposable containers be the ideal present? Whatever the situation, I promise you this: with a little thought, the perfect gift can brighten someone's day and be very meaningful!

If someone, however, is facing a life-threatening illness, consider other options that might be more appropriate. Find out what might be helpful to the family, and consider ways you can really make a difference. From cooking to carpooling, your assistance with kind deeds and helpful errands will make a huge difference. Whatever the situation, there is no substitute for sending your feelings and thoughts for their well-being. So consider what that person means to you. Have you told them how much you love them lately? Don't resist or postpone any thoughtful gesture.

The following get-well gifts range from humorous to helpful. They also include ways you can express your sympathy and, when necessary, send your condolences. Whatever you do, choose a gift or gesture that will both be memorable and express your heartfelt concern in a purposeful and creative way.

CALL IN A JESTER! For anyone who is facing a challenging illness or any difficult situation at all, call 1-800-9-JESTER and order *The Jester Has Lost His Jingle*, written and illustrated by David Saltzman. This spectacular children's book tells the tale of a jester who is worried that the world has lost its sense of humor. While the author, a courageous and talented Yale graduate, lost his life to Hodgkin's disease, his dedicated parents carried out their promise to see the book through to publication. It has now touched the hearts of hundreds of thousands of readers and brought an uplifting message to all those who encounter it. You can also order the Jester & Pharley doll from this company to go along with the book. It will be a gift that the entire family will treasure.

IT'S THE LITTLE THINGS THAT COUNT. Know someone laid up in the hospital, worried about all that needs to be done at home? Take those worries away. Hire a cleaning service to spruce up the house or someone to mow the yard—or do it yourself. These may not be the kind of gifts you can wrap up and present, but they'll be most welcome.

SEND YOUR WARMEST WISHES. Send a comfy afghan or throw blanket to someone who is suffering from a cold or the flu or is confined to bed. Your note could read: "Under the weather? I hope you'll feel better under this and get well soon. Warmest wishes for your speedy recovery!"

ALL SCREAM FOR ICE CREAM! Remember when you were a kid, and you thought it'd be great to have your tonsils out because everyone said you could eat all the ice cream you wanted? Go back to the good ol' days and deliver the perfect gift. Take a selection of smooth, rich ice creams in both familiar and exotic flavors to a friend who's recovering. If they're into low-fat foods, select a lower-fat ice cream or frozen yogurt. Add a note that says, "I'll scream if you don't get better soon!"

MUSIC TO SNOOZE BY. Check out your local music store for a great selection of relaxing music. Consider choices that soothe the soul or even music that imitates sounds in nature. Make sure they have a cassette or CD player so that your gift will be enjoyed, or consider giving a portable radio with headphones for a prolonged stay in bed.

NO BONES ABOUT IT: THEY'LL LOVE THIS PRESENT. For a kid with a broken bone, send a note that says, "Now that you've had the X rays, how about some X-ray vision?" Attach your note to a selection of Superman comic books or any superhero-themed gift.

HOPE YOU'LL POP UP SOON. Rise to the occasion and send these sentiments with a fabulous popcorn gift from Thatcher's Special Popcorn. Call 1-800-926-CORN (2676) and order organic gourmet popcorn from Thatcher's. Choose from a variety of fifteen all-natural flavors including caramel corn, fat-free and low-fat caramel, white cheddar cheese, sour cream and onion, macadamia, or cookies 'n' cream.

TICKLED PINK. Send a beautiful bouquet of perfectly pink roses or carnations to a friend or family member who is ill. Add a note saying, "We'd be tickled pink to hear you're feeling better. Get well soon."

'TIS THE SEASON. Depending on what fruit is in season, fill a basket with a healthy selection and add a note:

- Peaches: "Hope you're feeling peachy soon."

- Nectarines: "I'd stick my nec out for you any day of the week!"

- Apples: "An apple a day . . . hope this helps!"

- Oranges: "Orange you feeling better yet?"

- Pears: "Hope to pear up with you soon. Get well quick!"

- Bananas: "Sorry you slipped and fell. . . . Hope you'll soon be up and well!"

- Assortment of fruit: "Assorted wishes for your quick recovery."

FOOD, GLORIOUS FOOD. Often, when word gets around that a friend is ill, people are there immediately, bearing gifts of food—from casseroles to cakes. The idea of helping to feed the family while a member is sick is quite meaningful. It takes away the daily planning and preparation of meals, which can be a great relief when one is not well. Another option is to provide "freezer pleaser" meals that can be pulled out of the freezer and heated when needed. That kind of get-well gift is especially appreciated by people such as new parents, who will have their hands full for a while.

WHODUNIT? Add a little suspense to a get-well gift and give a copy of your favorite mystery or thriller. Include a note that says, "It's a mystery why nice people like you get sick. Hope everything gets solved real soon!"

SOMETHING TO LAUGH ABOUT. Cheer up a bedridden friend with a couple of funny movies on video. Your note could read, "Laughter is the best medicine. Watch two a day, and call me tomorrow."

FOOD FOR THOUGHT. Bear the gift of words and give a copy of *Simple Abundance*, by Sarah Ban Breathnach (Warner Books, 1995). This book is packed with endless wisdom especially suited for women who wish to live by their own lights. With an inspiration for every day of the year, you'll find encouraging words for any woman trying to balance life and make the most of every day.

DON'T STAY HOME WITHOUT IT! Purchase a copy of the Direct Marketing Association's *Great Catalog Guide* and give it to someone who is confined to bed for quite a while. This fabulous catalog resource lists toll-free numbers and descriptions of catalogs of all kinds. The guide also includes tips on shopping and consumer protection via shopping by telephone, mail, or computer. A perfect gift for the homebound person who has a love for shopping. Send a $3.00 check or money order to: Consumer Services Dept., Direct Marketing Association, P.O. Box 33033, Washington, D.C. 20033-0033.

THEY'LL MELT OVER THIS GIFT. Flavored ice pops and ice cream bars now come in every shape, size, and color. From fat-free bars to ones shaped like cartoon characters, there's something for everyone. Both kids and adults love them, so fill their freezer with a creative assortment.

FOCUS ON LIFE. When someone has passed away, one of the most meaningful gifts you can give is to focus on the beauty of that person's life. For example, write about a good deed he did or perhaps something she taught you. Express how he made life better for others or how she influenced you in a special way. Your words of comfort will be appreciated more than you'll ever know.

MAKE A DONATION. I have always found a donation to a non-profit organization to be the perfect present to wish someone a speedy recovery or to honor a loved one's memory. Choose a cause that you feel will be meaningful to them, or even a charity you wholeheartedly support. Most nonprofit organizations have a toll-free number or local telephone number and can be easily reached to inquire about donation procedures and acknowledgment cards.

SUIT THEM TO A TEA. When I'm not feeling well, I always turn to a soothing cup of hot tea to lift my spirits, even if it won't cure me. Many people feel the same way about tea. Consider giving a whimsical teapot with a selection of flavored teas. Add a note that says, "It'd suit me to a tea if you get well soon!"

THE PERFECT BASKET! Call 1-800-440-2131 and order a catalog from Giftcorp, a distinctive gourmet food and gift-giving company that provides tasteful options for all occasions. These baskets are beautifully presented and ideal to send as get-well gifts or as an appropriate way to express your condolences. No refrigeration is required of any of their food products, and they ship within twenty-four hours. You can also visit their Web site at www.giftsbygiftcorp.com.

THOSE ACHES AND PAINS. Consider someone's aches and pains when searching for the perfect present. From migraine headaches to excess stress, check out your options for great gifts that just might provide some healthful benefit or physical comfort: a massage, yoga classes, or even a trip to a spa are all great options. You might even give a membership to a related organization that disseminates information about their condition, or investigate available products to give them relief. For example, call 1-800-290-2225 and order the Relax the Back catalog, filled with products that provide lifestyle solutions for back pain relief.

GAMES PEOPLE PLAY. Consider putting together a selection of games that are easy to play in bed. From Mr. Potato Head to magnetic games like ticktacktoe to Old Maid and other card games, select age-appropriate games that will make time fly. And don't forget the grown-ups: there is a wonderful selection of games adults will enjoy playing, from high-tech versions of solitaire to word games and crossword puzzles. Add a note that says, "Hope your next move is right out of bed—feel better soon!"

GIVE A GIFT FROM THE HEART. When my beloved grandmother Pauline died, my mother's friend Ardie Rodale, author of *Gifts of the Spirit* (Daybreak Books, Rodale Press, 1997), sent Mom a cut-glass prism with the following words of comfort: "Please hang this prism in a window where the sun shines through. At unexpected times when rainbows dance it is a happy reminder of your mother's vibrant energy that will always live happily in the hearts of all those of you who will love her forever."

MAKE A BEDSIDE BASKET. Fill a basket with an assortment of presents that will help make being in bed a little more enjoyable. Consider aromatic candles, a new nightgown, videotapes, a few magazines, and anything that will make bed rest easier to take.

GO TO ANY LENGTHS TO SAY "GET WELL." Call Supergram at 1-800-3-BANNER (322-6637) and send a large custom banner that unrolls right out of a gift box that will arrive by mail. On eleven-inch-wide continuous paper with up to forty-eight characters (include spaces), you can spread your get-well wishes in a great big way! These banners, with additional features such as laminating services, are perfect for anyone who is hospital-bound or whom you want to cheer up in a totally creative and clever way! Include a message that says, "We'd go to any length to say 'Get well soon!'" or, "Hope your recovery doesn't take too long!"

Housewarming and Good-bye Presents $\underline{16}$

Whether someone is coming or going, leaving town or moving in, it's a meaningful time to express your feelings. From warm welcomes to sentimental farewells, the act of relocating or changing addresses is a special time for gift giving. Whether they are moving to a new city or just around the corner, the ideas in this chapter are bound to "transport" anyone on your gift list.

When giving a good-bye or housewarming present, your concern for another's happiness can be displayed in myriad ways. First of all, consider what might really be meaningful. Are they leaving friends and family behind? Is this a big career move? Are they moving into their first house?

When someone moves, they usually leave excess stuff behind and scale down their belongings. So, consider items that they will really enjoy and appreciate. While a crystal vase might be the ideal present for one friend who just moved into a new house, it might be a dust collector for another.

Put on your thinking cap and don't just grab the first thing you see. If you select a present that is really special, not only will they appreciate and love it, but it will stay with them throughout the years and be a reminder of you.

Housewarming Presents

CLUTTER BUSTERS TO THE RESCUE! Call 1-800-733-3532 and the Container Store catalog will arrive to your rescue with one-stop shopping for everything under the sun to help you get organized. From household gadgets to closet and drawer organizers of every description, the Container Store has a super solution for every space-saving need. Give a gift certificate with their catalog, or fill up a colorful trash can or laundry basket with something useful to help organize every nook and cranny.

READY AND LABEL. Personalized labels are a big hit for anyone with a change of address. Call 1-800-458-7999 and order a catalog from Colorful Images, which features one of the largest assortments of creative personalized address labels, note pads, and other decorative items. Choose your favorite images from over 1,100 labels, including every imaginable theme, character, holiday, and subject area. Consider ordering labels for each family member for a really spectacular gift that will be put to good use.

PANTRY PLEASERS. Can't think of anything they need for the new house? A wonderful housewarming gift is to stock up one of their pantries with items that are really useful. From a basket of soups in the wintertime to a fabulous selection of herbs and spices to a selection of necessary paper products including napkins and paper towels, they'll love your pantry-pleasing gift.

MATCH IT UP. When someone moves into a new home, they usually have items that aren't updated or that don't match the new surroundings. Find out what objects they'd really love in a new color or style. From a toaster that blends in with their kitchen color scheme to monogrammed hand towels that compliment their powder room, you'll find a wealth of ideas revealed by checking out which items need a new look.

NO HOME SHOULD BE WITHOUT IT! Call 1-800-626-6488 and order the Frontgate catalog, exclusively designed to enhance your life at home. Filled with an array of well-made products that serve every need you might have at home, it's the perfect resource for products that make the living easy as well as easy on the eye! Whether you are searching for the perfect pool items, the latest high-tech gadget, or personalized address plaques, there's something for every home in this catalog.

CALLING ALL COUNTRY LOVERS. For anyone on your gift list who has a country home or just loves a little country flair, call 1-800-331-3602 and order the Country House catalog. This charming catalog is filled with many exclusive items such as reproductions of antique tea sets, cookie jars, boxes, toys, signage, and dolls. From exclusive candles and potpourri to a wide range of decorative accessories with warm and colorful primitive patterns, you'll discover a world of country creations awaiting your call.

BALLARD TO THE RESCUE. Call 1-800-367-2775 and order a catalog from Ballard Designs. Filled with accents for the home and garden, this tempting resource is jam-packed with outstanding presents that will warm up any house. From handcrafted furniture to a fabulous presentation of decorative accessories, Ballard Designs presents a unique collection of antique reproductions and artistic designs.

GIFTS GALORE. Call 1-888-249-4155 and order the Crate & Barrel catalog, filled with a wonderful selection of accessories, gadgets, functional kitchen items, and decorative objects certain to enhance any home. Be sure to check out their gift certificates, gift registry, and endless options for pleasing that special someone who just moved into a new home. You could also show your friend the catalog and let him or her make a wish list.

HOME, STYLISH HOME. Call 1-800-922-5507 and order the Pottery Barn catalog, which features a wide variety of stylish accessories, decorative items, and even furniture. At a loss for what to choose? Call and order a gift certificate, which will arrive via first-class mail in a special gift package that includes a copy of their latest catalog. The Pottery Barn also offers monogramming services for designated linens and towels.

Good-Bye Presents

NEVER CAN SAY GOOD-BYE. If you don't want to say good-bye to someone who's moving to another city, give them a present that prepares them for your visit! Purchase a book about things to do in that town. You can also call the Chamber of Commerce in that city and request a newcomer's packet. Wrap up all your information in a basket with a subscription to the city's newspaper or a popular local magazine. Not only will you keep them informed about what's happening in their new part of the world, but you can also let them know you're helping them prepare for sightseeing on your first visit!

DINING OUT. Most major cities have Zagat's restaurant guides, or some other comprehensive guide to the local restaurant scene. Arrange a gift certificate to one of the highly recommended dining spots for friends moving to a new town or city. Call the owners of the restaurant ahead of time and arrange for a special welcome dessert or handshake from the maitre'd to welcome them to town!

Thank-You Presents

*G*ifts of thanks are a wonderful expression of gratitude. Thank-you presents are an excellent way to let others know how much their thoughtfulness has meant to you. Also, these tokens of appreciation mark one good deed with another in return.

There are dozens of occasions and situations where a thank-you present is appropriate. Whether someone goes out of his or her way for your sake, extends hospitality, entertains you, or does some act of kindness on your behalf, "Thank you" is a meaningful expression that shows that the effort has not been wasted. Your thank-you acknowledges those kind actions and validates the giver's time and energy.

Bearing a present as you arrive at someone's house for dinner or sending a thank-you note or present immediately after a visit is important. It's not enough to just strip the bed and put the laundry in a pile; when someone entertains you a thank-you note is necessary, and in most situations even a small token of your affection is highly appropriate. But don't despair—even when you don't know what to do, there are many creative ways to say thank you.

Two of the most meaningful thank-yous I ever received were in the way of words from our children. After a day of running errands, our eleven-year-old daughter, Ali, said to me while we were driving in the car, "Mom, have I told you how much happiness you have given me?" My eyes welled up with tears and I knew that Ali had given me the perfect present of thanks. Another thank-you that meant the world to me was our son, Justin's, poem about me. His words touched my heart as he thanked me for being such a wonderful mom.

Present your gift of thanks creatively and, if appropriate, with a witty note. Words and feelings add another dimension that makes a present even more memorable. Here are some suggestions to help you get started.

THANKS FOR THE MEMORIES. Photos are memories you can hold in your hand and look at over the years. If someone has done something nice for you that resulted in good memories—perhaps by allowing you to stay at their home or to use their vacation property—say "thanks" in a very personal way. Create a small album of photos you took while on that vacation, and share some of the special times you'll recall when you think back on it. Just get two copies made of all the photos you take on vacation, choose some that your friends would enjoy seeing, and arrange them in a photo album. Include fun captions and words of thanks to your hosts. If one photograph in particular stands out, enlarge it and put it in a frame to be hung in the house. For example, our son, Justin, took a photograph of a butterfly perched on a flower while we were at our aunt and uncle's beach house one summer. It was the perfect present and captured a spectacular moment they'll enjoy viewing all year round.

A THANK-YOU THEY'LL TREASURE. One of my favorite ways to thank someone who has invited me to stay at their home is to hide a few cards and presents in drawers in the room I stayed in and then send my host on a treasure hunt after I leave. From greeting cards to small boxes of candy or note cards, each little gift signifies your appreciation. You can also hide your presents in easy places to spot, like in the refrigerator or on their pillow. If there are young children in the family, they'll love getting clues with hints about where you hid your thanks.

THANKS FOR THE HOSPITALITY. Present your host and hostess with a welcome mat (choose a seasonal one, with a holiday scene or summer flowers on it, or have their initials custom-painted right in the center). Your note could read, "Thanks for making us feel so welcome."

LEADING THE WAY. Do you want to let the outgoing president of your club or association know how much you've appreciated his work? Present him with a fine leather steering-wheel cover for his car, along with a note saying, "You steered us in the right direction," or, "Thanks for being our driving force!"

AN ORGANIZED THANK-YOU! Has someone put a lot of effort into organizing a meeting, retreat, reunion, or other event? Buy them some organizing accessories for their home or office, such as a desk set or a basket filled with organizers. The note could say, "To the best organizer around," or, "This organization appreciates you!"

THANKS FOR THE SUPPORT. Has someone shared some kind words that gave you the strength you needed to accomplish your goal? Let them know how much those words meant to you. Give them a copy of a favorite CD or cassette tape with a note explaining, "Your encouragement was music to my ears."

A SONG OF THANKS. There are dozens of songs that say thank you, so visit your local music store and select an appropriate CD or cassette. Choose from songs like "Thank You for Being a Friend," and add a note that says, "Think of me whenever you hear this song!"

BRIGHTEN THEIR DAY! Give candles and a beautiful set of candlestick holders with a note that says, "Thanks for helping me see there was light at the end of the tunnel." Need a resource for this illuminating present? Call 1-800-CANDLES and order an Illuminations catalog, filled with a magnificent array of candles in every shape, size, and color including a great selection of aromatherapy and herbal choices.

HAS SOMEONE HELPED YOU TACKLE A BIG JOB? Send a football or football jersey with a note that says, "I couldn't have tackled this job without you! Thanks for being such a team player!"

SAY "THANKS" TO SOMEONE WHO HELPED YOU OUT IN A CRUNCH. Call 1-800-452-8162 and request a catalog from Mrs. London's Confections, which specializes in handmade buttercrunch toffees. Made from only the finest ingredients in small three-pound batches, Mrs. London's award-winning buttercrunch has been highly recommended as one of the best mail-order foods available. Made with love, the lineup of flavors includes English Toffee Crunch, Milk Chocolate Peanut Crunch, and Coffee Lover's Crunch.

A GARDEN OF THANKS. Here's a thank-you that will brighten things up! Call 1-800-503-9624 and order a gift certificate from White Flower Farm. Specify the amount you want to send and they'll deliver a certificate, handsomely packaged to you or directly to the recipient with a copy of their current catalog, which is filled with more than one thousand annuals, perennials, bulbs, shrubs, and houseplants. What could be easier?

SWEETEN YOUR THANK YOU. Looking for a really delicious way to say thank you? Send a world famous Carnegie Deli cheesecake anywhere in the continental United States. Call 1-800-334-5606 and order this creamy cheesecake baked at the Carnegie Delicatessen & Restaurant in New York City.

THANK-YOU GIFTS GALORE. Call 1-800-525-9291 and order the Walter Drake catalog, which is filled with hundreds of items that will be enjoyed throughout the year. This well-known catalog has a wide variety of wonderful gifts, including personalized stationery and unique household products and health-care items. A favorite present I order often are address labels that I have personalized with messages for different occasions, such as "Happy Holidays! Love, Phyllis and Jack." This label is perfect for gift wrapping in a flash and a luxury to have on hand!

THANKS BY THE LOAF. Say thank you to some special friends with the good, old-fashioned gift of bread. Deliver hot fresh-baked bread with a note that says, "Any way you slice it, you're the best."

A THANKFUL HEART. Celebrate Thanksgiving by giving thanks, and then sending your thanks, too. Just before Thanksgiving, rather than sending out holiday greeting cards, consider sending out Thanksgiving cards offering your thanks to friends, family, coworkers, and people you appreciate all year long. Not only will you beat the holiday rush, but your greetings will be memorable.

FORGET ME NOT. If you stay at someone's home, find out what their favorite flower is and then leave the house filled with flowers. Or, if flowers aren't their thing, a bottle of wine or champagne in the refrigerator will get your thank-you across.

Teacher Presents 18

I am reminded over the years how special many of my teachers were. Perhaps you can think of a teacher or mentor you really loved and valued, too. One of my favorites was Mrs. Harris, with whom I am still in touch. Another was Mr. Pepe, my seventh-grade teacher, and after all these years I made sure he knew it by writing him a letter. He wrote me back a letter that made my day!

It has always been my goal to thank my children's teachers and make sure my children understand the importance of a thank-you. From a letter to a gift that a child makes, whatever you choose to do to say thank you will mean a lot to a teacher. The following ideas will help you choose gifts for teachers you know and adore, and hopefully will let them know how much their efforts are really appreciated!

LET EVERYONE HAVE A HAND IN THIS GIFT! Here's a gift every student can contribute to. Purchase a simple canvas tote bag, and have every child in the class use paint to make his or her handprint on the bag. Next, write each child's name under the appropriate print or let the children write their own names with a fabric marker. Any teacher would love this bag because it's useful, and each time she picks it up, she will be reminded of the children she taught in that class. She'll also be amazed that the entire project was pulled off without her knowledge.

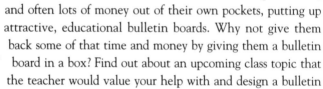

BECOME CHAIRMAN OF THE BOARD. Teachers spend hours, and often lots of money out of their own pockets, putting up attractive, educational bulletin boards. Why not give them back some of that time and money by giving them a bulletin board in a box? Find out about an upcoming class topic that the teacher would value your help with and design a bulletin board to go with it. Buy all the supplies needed, cut out any letters that will be needed, and do all the other time-consuming work required. Present the teacher with everything required to make it and staple it up to the bulletin board.

TEACHER'S CHOICE. Nothing goes over better with a teacher than a really useful gift certificate at a favorite store. With each student contributing to the gift, you'll be able to make it significant. Plus, your teacher will be able to choose something she's always wanted. Be sure to make a great match when selecting the store. For example, if he's a music teacher, find out where he buys his favorite music. Or, if she teaches English and is an avid reader, discover where she loves to buy books.

I'VE SEEN THE LIGHT. Give a good-quality flashlight for the teacher to keep in his or her car in case of emergencies. You could also give a book light, a night-light, or anything that lights up. Have your child enclose a note that says, "Thanks for enlightening me."

WILD ABOUT A TEACHER? Does your class have a teacher who is wild about the environment or wildlife? He might appreciate a donation given in his name to a wildlife conservation group or even the local zoo. Explain the donation in a note and be sure to express the thought that "We're wild about you!"

FOCUS ON YOUR TEACHER. Present the teacher with a disposable camera. Add a note that says, "Thank you for helping me develop a picture-perfect year. You always kept me in focus!"

TAKE NOTE OF THIS. The array of note cards is endless, and you're bound to find some that reflect your teacher's interests or personality. Another option is a supply of sticky notes with funny sayings on them, which teachers can use to make comments on graded papers. Present the gift with a card that reads, "It was a notable class, thanks to you!"

THE QUOTABLE TEACHER. Choose a special book of quotes for your teacher that he or she might appreciate. You could also find a few quotes that describe your teacher and write them in a decorative book, giving credit to the coiner of the phrase. Or add a note that says, "Talk about famous words worth repeating—you wrote the book on it!"

YOU SUIT ME TO A TEA! Give your teacher a selection of flavored teas from all over the world. Visit your local grocery store and choose exotic flavors. Add a note that says, "You suit me to a tea. You're a totally tea-riffic tea-cher!"

MAKE IT WEARABLE. No matter what subject your instructor teaches, you're bound to find a T-shirt that features related graphics. For an art teacher, a Monet print; for a math teacher, Einstein. Most cities have a T-shirt shop or gift shop that displays a wide variety of designs.

A NIGHT ON THE TOWN. Teachers are just like the rest of us: they also enjoy getting away from the job occasionally. Give your teacher a night off with a gift certificate to a restaurant, or present him with tickets to a concert, show, or sporting event you think he'd enjoy. Your card could read, "It's time for recess. You deserve a break."

THIS TEACHER HAS CLASS. For a teacher who appreciates the finer things in life, fill up a basket with gourmet goodies. Everyone in the class could bring one item and you could surprise your teacher with a fabulous basket filled to the brim.

MUFFIN BUT GOOD THINGS. Call 1-800-742-2403 and order a box of Suzanne's Mail Order Muffins. Check out the lineup of delicious muffins, including chunky apple, chocolate cream cheese, and even low-fat lovelies. Add a note saying "There's muffin like a great teacher!"

A SIGNATURE GIFT. Ceramics are very popular these days and are easily created at a do-it-yourself studio. Or, visit the school's art teacher and check what resources are available for creating a one-of-a-kind work of art. Choose a platter, teapot, or ready-made item and prepare it for glazing. Then on a day the teacher is out of the room, encourage each child to paint his or her name on the object (use special pottery glaze). Have it fired and present it to the teacher with love from the class.

Career and Hobby Presents

*H*obby and special-interest gifts are a wonderful way to give a present that will really be appreciated. They also show that you've gone to great lengths to consider the recipient's favorite things in life. From writing to woodworking, golf to gourmet cooking, everyone has something they enjoy doing, and this chapter will assist you in giving a gift that really hits the nail on the head!

To get you started on the right track, consider yourself an investigative reporter and get the facts by asking all the right questions. Does she love to cook? Is he an avid reader of mystery novels? Does he live for sports? Does he favor a round of golf, or is he a fisherman at heart? Is she an avid art collector? Does she love to run or collect fine wines? Is he a lawyer? Is she a doctor? Whatever the career, hobby, or interest, you can find related items that make perfect presents.

However, if you find yourself at a shopping standstill, look up the area of interest in the business section of the telephone book or your yellow pages and do some homework. There might be an association that focuses on this topic and could refer you to great gifts or a local store selling related items. You'll be surprised what a little research will uncover. With a little thought, you'll be on your way to giving a gift that will be absolutely perfect. In the meantime, here are some ideas to help you get going!

 FOR MUSIC LOVERS ONLY. Call 1-800-414-4010 and order a free catalog from the Music Stand. This company specializes in a terrific selection of gifts with a performing-arts theme, including coffee mugs, tote bags, and clothing. Whether you're looking for a gift for a professional musician or a starstruck drama student, you'll find something here. Or, find out what music the person listens to and purchase a long-awaited CD release.

CALLING ALL READERS. Call 1-800-544-0880 and order a copy of Levenger's catalog, filled with tools for serious readers dedicated to a well-read life. From prestigious pens and desk accessories to monogrammed leather goods, this catalog is a real page-turner full of fabulous gift ideas for anyone who loves to read or write.

GIFTS IN FOCUS. If you have a photo buff on your hands and want to select a picture-perfect gift, call 1-800-643-WOLF (9653) and order the Wolf Camera catalog. It's filled with the best-quality photographic equipment and accessories, and you'll be able to focus on a great gift that will be appreciated for years.

COMPUTE THIS GIFT. For the avid computer user, investigate the world of gift possibilities, including thematic screen savers and personalized mouse pads created from a favorite photograph. Or, check out and find a reputable computer expert who makes house or office calls, and give a gift certificate for an emergency computer crash!

SUBSCRIPTION TO SUCCESS. No matter what the hobby, chances are there is at least one magazine, and there are probably more, devoted to that particular interest. A subscription to such a periodical would be a welcome gift—provided you make sure he or she doesn't already subscribe to it!

WORDS OF THANKS. Here's a gift you'll be thanked for time and time again. Know a wordsmith? Whether it is someone who writes for a living or someone who simply enjoys putting words on paper in notes to friends, crossword puzzles, or the occasional poem, a dictionary can be just the thing. Go for the most up-to-date, complete dictionary you can find. Other possibilities include a rhyming dictionary, a reverse dictionary (for those times when you know the definition, but can't recall the word), a slang dictionary, or a thesaurus. Whichever book you give, your recipient is likely to turn to it often. Your card could read, "It'd take all of the words in this book to express how special you are!"

HIGH-TECH TOYS. Check out the vast array of high-tech gadgets for everyone on your gift list. Learn how to use the item and give with it a lesson from yours truly. Include extra batteries and make sure it's something they will really value. From cellular telephones for the car to electronic telephone and address books, there's something for everyone.

THE END OF THE RAINBOW. Many quilters stockpile fabric, figuring they'll find just the right project for it sometime in the future. They love receiving new fabric in a range of colors—even a variety of whites. To them, it's a gift full of possibilities. If you're giving fabric, just remember that most quilters like 100 percent cotton, and they need at least one-half yard of any material to have enough to work with. Or if your gift list includes someone who loves to sew, fill up a sewing basket with new scissors, spools of thread, a pincushion, and assorted needles for every sewing occasion.

HERE'S A REAL HIT! Call 1-800-WE-PITCH (1-800-937-4824) and order the Baseball Express and Softball Express catalogs, filled with a broad selection of high-quality baseball and softball equipment, gloves, balls, clothing, shoes, bats, and training equipment—just name it. Check out their personalized products for the baseball enthusiast as well as replicas of pro-team jerseys for a die-hard fan. Gift certificates are also available for the player who has everything, or just in case you aren't sure what your baseball fanatic would consider a real hit!

ANIMAL LOVERS. If the person on your gift list has a pet, then choose a gift for the animal. From monogrammed dog beds to special leashes that make dog walking easier to products that entertain a curious cat, investigate the world of possibilities for a pet lover's gift. Need a resource? Call Doctors Foster and Smith at 1-800-562-7169 and order this 140-page high-quality affordable pet-supply catalog with supplies approved by practicing veterinarians. Or, if you have a horse lover on your list, check out the Back in the Saddle catalog by calling 1-800-865-2478.

JUST NAME IT. Every well-appointed desk deserves a distinguished nameplate that says who works there. Visit your local printer or trophy shop and check out the available resources for custom-ordering an engraved nameplate. They come in dozens of styles and are a perfect present for anyone on your gift list who spends most of the day behind a desk.

AN ARTIST AT HEART. Investigate the media your artist at heart enjoys and choose some new supplies that will enhance his or her next creation. Or, choose a book all about this person's favorite artist. For an art collector, select a book about someone whose prints he or she actually owns. For a super selection of quality art materials and other accessories for art lovers, call 1-800-447-8192 and order the Dick Blick Art Materials catalog for a colorful selection of gifts.

BACK TO EARTH. If you have a garden lover on your list, give a gift certificate to your local garden center. Or, order the Burpee Gardens catalog by calling 1-800-283-5159. This catalog is filled with over three hundred different vegetables and four hundred varieties of flowers, plus fruit trees, shrubs, bulbs, bedding plants, and garden accessories. Gift certificates are also available in case you aren't sure what gift will grow on your gardener!

DRIVEN TO PERFECTION. Many people have a strong affinity for their car. They may spend a great deal of time in it but stop short of adding some of the extras that would make it more comfortable. Investigate what types of accessories are available for a loved one's car by calling a local car dealer and inquiring about additional products they might sell. You'll find special license plates, customized key chains, toy replicas, and other special gadgets personalized exclusively for the car your friend drives! Mercedes-Benz, for example, has a magnificent catalog collection. Call 1-800-FOR-MERCEDES and check out those miles of smiles!

GREAT GIFTS FOR GOOD SPORTS. The sporting goods enthusiast will love any item in the L.L. Bean spring or summer sporting catalog, filled with sporting goods for the family. Call 1-800-221-4221 for a terrific resource filled with great products of every imaginable description. If you have a fly-fishing fanatic on your gift list and want a gift that will really fly, order the L.L. Bean fly-fishing catalog. Or, call 1-800-541-3541 and check out the wide selection of Orvis Travel catalogs, jam-packed with sporting goods, clothing, items for travel, and accessories.

LOOK WHAT'S COOKING. Searching for the perfect present for a gourmet cook or at-home chef? Call 1-800-338-3232 and order the Chef's catalog, filled with professional restaurant equipment for the home chef. A thousand and one unique gourmet kitchenware items and a personal shopper and registry are available.

FOR THE GOLFER WHO HAS EVERYTHING. Call 1-800-348-4646 and order British Links, a catalog that specializes in fine golf art, gifts, and collectibles. You'll discover a fabulous collection of accessories, books, money clips, watches, mugs, hats, wall and desktop art, all in the theme of golf. An exciting selection of presents for the golfer who has almost everything.

GIFTS FOR THE AVID GOLFER. From a new golf shirt to a favorite brand of golf balls, golfers will tell you right up front to consider the basics. To get a really great gift, you are better off asking the golfer what he or she wants! Each golfer has individual preferences, and whatever works best for his or her game is best! Just in case you want to give a surprise, lessons are highly rated for a beginner, a golf shirt is always appreciated, high-quality golf balls are considered a luxury, and an avid golfer would enjoy a golf clinic conducted by leading professionals. Call a statewide golf organization or a nearby club for information about special opportunities such as this one. However, if you're still at a loss, consider a gift certificate. Check out the Austad's Golf catalog by calling 1-800-759-4653, or call Edwin Watts Golf Shops Pro-Line Golf Equipment at 1-800-874-0146 for two well-known resources filled with a wide variety of golf equipment and accessories your golfer will definitely appreciate.

BOOK IT. If you can't figure out the perfect gift to give your uncle who collects glass marbles, your friend who is interested in twentieth-century furniture, or your nephew who collects stamps, check out your local bookstore. Don't despair! You're sure to find the perfect book all about their specific interest.

CALLING ALL GARDENERS. Call 1-800-776-3336 and order a Smith & Hawken catalog, which specializes in flowering baskets, gardening products, tools, garden furniture, accessories, and an entire range of gardening supplies. Talk about a down-to-earth present: this company has you covered!

A RUNAWAY SUCCESS. Perhaps you have a runner on your list? Check out the leading books on running, or consider a gift certificate to the runner's favorite running store. From shirts to shorts, socks to shoes, there's a huge selection of gifts for the runner who enjoys running in style and comfort. Or, if you're on the run and don't have time to shop, call 1-800-551-5558 and order the Road Runner Sports catalog, filled with a complete selection of running and fitness shoes and apparel. Gift certificates are available and always a huge success.

BEAR WITH US. The Vermont Teddy Bear Co. (1-800-829-2327) sells wonderful stuffed-toy bears dressed to represent different kinds of people and their interests. The recipient will love the idea of having a bear that does what he or she does, and you can even request that your order be personalized with any name! For the athletically inclined, sports bears range from an angler to a cheerleader, with a representative of most major sports—football, hockey, basketball, golf, and baseball—available. New this year, the Vermont Teddy Bear Co. now offers officially licensed NFL teddy bears. These bears are dressed in official team jerseys and even wear bear-sized Riddell helmets. Call and speak with a teddy bear counselor who will help you dress and design the optimum bear.

HELP FOR HOME MANAGERS. Here's the perfect present for anyone trying to manage the busiest room in the house. *Rosemary Brown's Big Kitchen Instruction Book* (Andrews McMeel, 1998) shows how to achieve terrific results in a reasonable amount of time. This 400-page kitchen encyclopedia contains all the information necessary to set up a kitchen and keep it running smoothly, plus over 500 recipes, dozens of menus, and a comprehensive reference section: everything you need to know from a real pro!

Business Presents 20

Regardless of the business you are in, you have probably discovered that expressing your appreciation to your clients, customers, or colleagues is meaningful and good business practice, too. It's always been my motto to make gratitude my business! In business, just as in our personal lives, presents play a special role. Most businesses go to great lengths during the holidays and on other special days to show their gratitude for a job well done or to solidify and nurture working relationships.

There are myriad types of business gifts, and choosing one that will represent your company's sentiments or your personal sentiments is easier than you think. When sending a gift from one business to another, the goal is to select something unique, something that sends a message, not just another corporate gift that gets lost in the shuffle. How much to spend on business presents varies, depending on your relationship and what you feel is appropriate. If someone has sent you a great deal of business, it's appropriate to spend more. There are no hard-and-fast rules, however, for what you should spend. The present should match your sentiments, but you can be creative without going into debt! Most businesses have strong views and sometimes policies about gift giving, and some don't allow employees to accept gifts valued at over a specific amount.

Having run a public-relations company with my husband for over sixteen years, I can certainly say we have given and received our share of presents. I have always marveled and long remembered the really creative presents we received. From a personalized leather briefcase to a magnificent silver clock to works of art and a box of juicy pears, each wrapped in gold foil, I've always been inspired by other businesses' thoughtfulness. In return, I love to give a present that will really surprise and delight. Business gifts should clearly be a reflection of the company, but the best presents reflect the taste of the recipient, too.

Corporate gift giving is much easier today, as most stores have dedicated a special department to these gifts. They are designed to help you choose appropriate gifts based on your budget and goals.

While there are no hard-and-fast rules for business gift giving, gifts often reflect a great deal of thoughtfulness that is long remembered after the gift is given. Since I love to give presents, I start thinking about what we will give our business contacts long before the holidays. The following ideas are wonderful examples no matter what business you're in. Consider also referring to other related chapters in this book for additional creative ideas.

READ ALL ABOUT IT. Consider running an ad in your local business magazine or newspaper to thank a company for doing such an outstanding job. Talk about great PR! They'll love your affirmation of their talents and appreciate the public display of your approval.

SUCCESSORIES. Call 1-800-554-6257 and order Successories, a fabulous catalog filled with success-oriented products, hundreds of motivational messages, and a wonderful assortment of desktop presents with an inspirational business slant. These products focus on reinforcing business goals and recognizing people's accomplishments and achievements. Consider their star awards, personalized with your star performer's name on it, framed posters, customized clocks, motivational books, screen savers and mouse pads in a variety of themes. Successories will help your company find a present that says thank you to your employees or best customers in an innovative way.

STICK WITH US! Consider giving self-adhesive labels or personalized Post-it notes with the user's or company's name on them. From pads of paper to personalized rubber stamps, visit an office supply store or stationery store and check out gifts that feature a business's name and address.

ONE OF A KIND. People always appreciate something that will beautify their lives. Select a work of art for your favorite Renaissance client or colleague. One of my favorite examples comes from dentists Goldstein, Garber & Salama, who send me gifts that make me smile—exquisite hand-blown perfume bottles. Thanks to them I started a magnificent collection. Check out what local artists and art galleries in your area are up to. From watercolors to pottery or sculpture, you can liven up anyone's work environment with art.

HEARTFELT THANKS. During the holidays, Certified Financial Planner Kay Shirley sent us an exotic flower, and I saved the lovely note that accompanied it. She had the note printed in script with her company name and the following poem written in colorful ink:

Thinking of you fondly
As the holiday season starts,
And wishing you the many joys
That make a happy heart!

HERE'S A JUICY IDEA! Call 1-800-776-7575 and order some of the sweetest fruit on Earth. Cushman's has provided outstanding fruit selections since 1945. Check out their limited-edition fruit, offered only at certain times of the year, including Cushman HoneyBells, which are the most delicious oranges you'll ever taste, and are available for only four short weeks in January. They even include a bib with these mouthwatering oranges. In December, a customized card arrives at the recipient's office or home and announces the special gift that's coming in January. Long after the other gifts have been eaten or forgotten, your gift will arrive. Include a note congratulating them on their sweet successes or wish them a sweet New Year. Cushman's also offers cantaloupes; huge, chin-dripping peaches; Bing cherries the size of golf balls (well, almost); and blueberries that are eye-popping. This company has something for everyone, depending on the season. Cushman's also offers a fine-fruit club with seasonal fruits delivered monthly.

DESKTOP DETAILS. Personalized desktop accessories are always a fabulous gift and can be found at most stores that have corporate gift departments. You can also purchase an item and then have a personalized brass plaque added. Check out trophy stores or companies that personalize and engrave items and you'll probably find a wide variety of choices. From desktop nameplates to clocks and desk protectors, consider all your options. For a great resource, call 1-800-718-8808 and order the Lizell catalog for home and office, which features a variety of accessories, pens, and executive gifts.

ROSS-SIMONS TO THE RESCUE. For one-stop shopping, call Ross-Simons at 1-800-556-7376 and order their world-famous catalog. For business gift giving, call the same number and ask for their corporate division for a unique and distinctive selection. Their trained representatives will assist you in finding the perfect present. Great ideas include paperweights, magnifying glasses, clocks, personalized stationery products, desk sets, sterling letter openers, and more.

TO THE SWEET SMELL OF SUCCESS. Call 1-800-64-JINIL for delectable candy and gifts. *Jinil au Chocolat* provides chocolate gifts of distinction to corporate clients. Consider a chocolate cellular phone with your telephone number on it, chocolate computers with logos on the screens, personalized chocolate business cards, and much, much more. This company can personalize anything in chocolate or customize a gift for a specific event or theme.

A REFILLABLE PRESENT. Here's a terrific idea for a business you visit or work with often. Order a candy jar and have a sticker made that says, "It's a treat working with you!" or, "To the sweetest colleagues on Earth!" Add your company name and number, and each time you visit, bring a refill for the candy jar. Just watch how happy everyone is to see you!

WE'D GO TO GREAT LENGTHS FOR YOU. If your company likes to give small tokens of appreciation to lots of clients or customers, here's a clever idea. Visit a hardware store, purchase inexpensive retractable measuring tapes, and fit the objects with personalized stickers that say, "We'd go to great lengths for your success . . . (add your company's name and telephone number)!"

JUST ASK. When giving an employee a gift, most employees know exactly what they'd like and usually aren't too shy to answer "money" or "a gift certificate." Be sensitive to their wants and likes—some may want a gift certificate to a spa, others to a favorite department store. Add a letter of appreciation for specific things they have done that you value. Words of sincere praise mean a lot, since we all too often forget to express our gratitude in day-to-day life.

MIND THEIR BUSINESS. Here's a great gift to help anyone keep business cards on hand. Purchase a business-card holder and have it personalized. From leather to silver, you'll find a style suitable for any businessperson on your list.

DON'T FORGET YOUR BOSS. Every boss wants to know that their employees are happy as clams working for them, so consider a gift that shows true thoughtfulness and give your boss a letter of thanks for hiring you. Write how you value your job, and be specific. Should you also desire to give your boss a token of your appreciation, consider his or her hobbies and taste. If your boss enjoys a particular sport, topic, or interest, purchase a book on that topic. If he or she loves a specific food, such as cookies, chocolate, or flavored coffee, focus on that. Personalized gifts are also a big hit, so check out stores that cater with customized gifts. Don't try to outdo other employees or match what the boss gave you. In this case, it's really the creative thought that counts!

TAKE A TOLL OFF YOUR SHOPPING. Call 1-800-426-8686 and purchase the AT&T National Toll-Free Directory—a fabulous guide to a great selection of products available by mail, featuring thousands of unique gift ideas at your fingertips. You'll find a wide selection of edible gifts, custom baskets, fabulous florists, custom imprinting, coffee companies, and more! You can also visit their Web site at www.tollfree.att.net.

KIDS ON BOARD? Our P.R. business often focuses on our clients' kids and selects special toys that are age-appropriate. Another favorite present-buying tactic for the holidays is to visit your local toy store in September and get their predictions for the top toys that will sell out during the holidays and buy them ahead of time for special clients' kids. These presents become very hard to find and you'll be a huge hit and a hero during the holidays!

TAKE THEM FOR A RIDE. Okay, you're bound to think this is totally extravagant, but nonetheless it's a real treat! A business I know surprised five of its clients by picking them up in a limousine and taking them out for an elegant lunch. Each client was presented with a beautiful pen and returned to his or her office in the afternoon.

TO A TEA-RIFFIC CLIENT. Add these words to a note and give an assortment of flavored teas for a wonderful present during the holidays or on any occasion. Assorted specialty teas are easily found in gift-boxed presentation, and they make a thoughtful present that will warm your client's heart!

TO SOMEONE WHO ALWAYS HAS NOVEL IDEAS. Add this saying to a card and combine it with a best-selling novel. If you do your homework and find out what your client enjoys reading, you'll be tops in his or her book, too!

IT'S BEAN WONDERFUL WORKING WITH YOU! Gourmet jelly or coffee beans combined with this quote will make a perfect present for someone who has a sweet tooth or is big on coffee. Put either in a coffee mug for a clever presentation.

NEIMAN MARCUS MARKS THE OCCASION. Call or check out the epicure department at any of the Neiman Marcus stores across the country. You'll find the most divine, scrumptious goodies packaged in beautiful presentations from all over the world. Check out their famous Australian apricots and Mrs. Prindable's Apples, which are covered in caramel and chocolate, for a business present that will be devoured upon receipt!

SEND A SONG. If a business sends you a referral or you wish to say thank you in a highly creative way, consider calling 1-800-SEND-A-SONG and send a song from a long list of musical choices with your own personalized, prerecorded, twenty-second message. Send-A-Song specializes in instantly sending a song or programming a time to send the song of your choice via telephone. They'll fax or send you a list of songs, and all you have to do is have a credit card ready for your purchase. From "Thank You for Being a Friend" to "Don't Worry, Be Happy" . . . there's a song for every business occasion.

BE OUR GUEST! Here's a ticket for finding the perfect present. If a hot musical, sports extravaganza, concert, or other spectacular event is coming to your city and tickets will be difficult to get, purchase a block of seats right when tickets go on sale. Send invitations ahead of time to your clients! If it's a family event, plan on inviting your clients' families. This present might cost a bundle, but it will be a surefire hit with your special customers or clients and a great way to entertain and give a present all in one.

STARBUCKS TO THE RESCUE. Call 1-800-782-7282 and order a catalog from Starbucks Coffee Company. You can liven up any dull coffeemaker with a specialty coffee gift sampler or coffee by the pound. You'll also find a wonderful assortment of coffee-related items including mugs, dipping cookies, and travel tumblers from Starbucks.

LOGO GIFTS. Call 1-800-440-2131 and investigate the clever selection of personalized logo gifts from Giftcorp. From incredible edibles packed in a canvas bag with your logo on it to chocolates tied up with ribbon printed with your company name, they'll go the extra mile that will make you and your clients smile! Favorite selections include scrumptious chocolate truffles, peachy peach buds, lemon shortbreads, decadent fudge brownies, butter toffee pretzels, fresh-baked cheese sticks, savory nuts, wine biscuits, and more. Check out this outstanding company on the Web at www.giftsbygiftcorp.com.

BAKE IT AND TAKE IT . . . Straight to your boss or favorite colleague and watch the reaction you get with home-baked goodies! Whether you are famous for your lemon pound cake made with pure butter, chocolate mint fudge, or baklava, you can sweeten anyone's day with some homemade treats. If you work with a fellow baker at heart, don't just give them the cake—fill a mixing bowl up with the recipe and a few of the ingredients so they can bake it themselves.

HAVE A REALLY HOT YEAR? Say thank you to your clients, suppliers, or colleagues with a present from the El Paso Chile Company. Call 1-888-4-SALSAS to order a catalog and send a selection of salsas, special sauces, and snacks to celebrate any season in a creative way. Add a note that says, "'Tis the season to celebrate you— we appreciate your business!"

FOR A CLIENT WHO TAKES THE CAKE! Call 1-800-422-5387 and order a cake from Cakes Across America. They'll arrange for the hand delivery of a freshly baked custom-decorated cake for any occasion, including corporate promotions. Fax them the company logo of your choice or a special message to decorate the cake. Bakers are standing by in every city across the country and are ready to deliver a delicious cake that your clients or customers will really eat up! For more information, check out their Web site at www.cakesacrossamerica.com.

IN THE NEWS. Do you know of a business or person who was recently featured in the news? Call 1-800-548-3993 and inquire about a fabulous service that will take any newspaper or magazine article, mount it on a wooden wall plaque, and preserve and protect it with laminated clear finish. Just tell them where and when the article appeared. They can also add an engraved plate that identifies the source and date or you can include a personalized message. This is a one-of-a-kind present that will "hang around" for a long time.

Presents for a Good Cause

21

*T*he best gifts in life come through the joy we gain from helping others. It amazes me how many wonderful opportunities we have to make a difference, and gift giving throughout the year can benefit a good cause. From special days to holidays, we have a multitude of ways to give back to our communities, whether it be through a donation or a gift that contributes to a nonprofit organization.

On a personal note, one of the greatest gifts you can give is your time and effort to help a good cause. You need not be rich in material wealth in order to give of yourself and help another. From lending an ear to someone who's bedridden to lending a hand to an organization that needs help, there are many possibilities if you want to give a gift straight from your heart.

Another way to make gift giving meaningful is to consider the organizations listed in this chapter, which represent only a small selection of the vast number of wonderful causes across the country. Seek out those opportunities in your area, or even initiate one, that might help a worthwhile cause you're passionate about. In the meantime, here are some wonderful choices for giving gifts that will brighten more lives than you could ever imagine!

A BOOK THAT MAKES A DIFFERENCE. Check out *Gifts That Make a Difference: How to Buy Hundreds of Great Gifts Sold Through Nonprofits,* by Ellen Berry (Foxglove Publishing, Dayton, Ohio, 1992). This book is jam-packed with a vast selection of 165 purposeful organizations that help protect animals, save the environment, fund disease research, help children, reduce hunger and homelessness, provide emergency relief, and support many other worthy causes.

MADE WITH CARE. CARE, the international relief and development agency, gives corporations and cause-minded shoppers a unique way of giving to the world's poorest families in developing countries. Made with Care merchandise includes specially designed home and fashion products available in stores across the country. Proceeds from the sale of Made with Care products help support CARE's relief and development programs overseas. For more information on Made with Care, call CARE at 1-800-521-CARE or visit their Web site at www.care.org. The following are a couple of the Made with Care manufacturers: Garden Botanika: 1-800-968-7842; Starbucks Coffee Company: 1-800-STARBUC.

TREE-MENDOUS WISHES. Call the Jewish National Fund Tree Certificate Department at 1-800-542-TREE (8733) and inquire about JNF's tree certificates, which announce that a tree has been planted in Israel in honor of the recipient. A beautiful certificate will be sent indicating the number of trees that have been planted in designated areas. Each tree costs $10.00 and helps the environment.

BASKETS THAT DO GOOD. Call 1-800-YAI-9914 or 516-338-4450 in New York Sate and request the YAI General Store, a mail-order catalog from which you can order a variety of innovative and personal gifts, which are sent right to your home. Launched by the YAI/National Institute for People with Disabilities, the catalog employs anywhere from three to thirty-five mentally challenged people, depending on the season. Choose from twenty-eight pre-designed baskets or gift packages, including the Family Feast; the Fiesta to Go; a basket for Fido or your favorite feline; the Snack Away Survival Kit, jam-packed with junk food; or the Recovery Kit, filled with chicken broth, crackers, and soft tissues. Or, how about a nylon knapsack filled with your choice of one full-sized board game, a giant-sized box of Cracker Jacks, and a box of microwave popcorn? There's a fabulous gift for everyone on your list!

SCOUT OUT THESE GIFTS! Call the Girl Scouts of America at 1-800-221-6707 and order their official catalog, which is filled with a huge selection of scouting merchandise and items that are perfect for your favorite scout all year long.

THE ELTON JOHN AIDS FOUNDATION. The Elton John AIDS Foundation was established in 1992 by Elton John, who serves as its chairman. Funding from the foundation encompasses a broad spectrum of direct patient-care services and prevention education for men, women, teenagers, children, infants, minorities, and entire families living with HIV/AIDS. Consider purchasing products for which a percentage of the retail price is donated to the Elton John AIDS Foundation. For example, call 1-800-CRISTAL and inquire about the magnificent Elton's Angel, which is a hand-signed and individually numbered Lalique crystal cherub, designed especially for Elton John. Or visit Slatkin & Co., New York; Neiman Marcus; or call 1-888-44-ELTON to order the Elton candle, which blends a bouquet of Elton's favorite flowers: hyacinth, freesia, jasmine, and rose, in a frosted-glass container with Elton John's signature in gold.

CIRCLES OF HOPE. Call 1-800-833-7769 or (909) 591-9122 in California and order a beautiful hand-made, all-natural Della Robbia Wreath from Boys Republic. Since 1940, these famous wreaths made by dis-advantaged youths to benefit their nonprofit school have made won-derful and heartwarming holiday decorations for home and office and wonderful gifts for family, friends, and coworkers. Colorful, fra-grant, and always fresh, these Boys Republic wreaths are made from lush California redwood or noble fir boughs. They sport the most succulent apples and lemons and a rich assortment of natural seed pods, pinecones, and evergreen sprigs. Orders are taken from early October through the first of December and then delivered during the holiday month throughout the United States and to all parts of the world. Get your order in early!

THE UNIVERSITY OF TEXAS M. D. ANDERSON CANCER CENTER CHILDREN'S ART PROJECT. For gifts and greeting cards designed by and benefiting young cancer patients, call 1-800-231-1580. Since its inception in 1973, the Children's Art Project has allocated more than $9.3 million in proceeds to fund an innovative variety of programs at the world-renowned M. D. Anderson Cancer Center. This hospital helps meet the educational, recreational, and emotional needs of cancer patients.

A RECIPE FOR SUCCESS. The Junior League is committed to promoting volunteerism, developing the potential of women, and improving communities through the effective action and leadership of trained volunteers. This almost one-hundred-year-old organiza-tion operates in 290 communities in the United States, Canada, Mexico, and Great Britain. For over fifty years, Junior Leagues have published community cookbooks to raise the funds to support their community work. One such book is *The Junior League Centennial Cookbook* (Main Street Books, Doubleday, 1996), containing over 750 recipes from more than two hundred Junior League cookbooks.

HEART-HEALTHY COOKBOOKS. The American Heart Association has produced several cookbooks full of healthful recipes that help others in two ways: the AHA benefits from the sale of the books, and the recipients benefit by having a way to improve their diets. The books, published by Times Books, a division of Random House, include a variety of titles. They range from *The American Heart Association Cookbook*, now in its fifth edition, with more than six hundred recipes, to *The American Heart Association Kids' Cookbook*, to help youngsters between the ages of eight and twelve learn to prepare their favorite foods in a healthful way. Other AHA cookbooks focus on low-fat, low-cholesterol foods; low-salt recipes; quick and easy recipes; and foods from around the world. If you can't find them at your local bookstore, you can order the AHA cookbooks from Random House at 1-800-793-2665 (credit card orders only).

THANK YOU FORE BEING YOU! Say thank you, happy birthday, or even "Congratulations on your retirement," to a golf lover on your gift list. Consider purchasing the American Lung Association's Golf Privilege Card, which is issued annually and includes discounts at golf courses in your area as well as neighboring states. Prices may vary by state, but the proceeds go to the American Lung Association. For details about the Golf Privilege Card, call 1-800-LUNG-USA.

AMERICAN DIABETES ASSOCIATION GIFTS. Call 1-800-608-4279 between August and December to receive a catalog full of holiday cards and gifts that benefit diabetes research. The American Diabetes Association has published its "Holiday Program" catalog for several years. The program was the idea of parents of children with diabetes, and all proceeds from the sale of catalog items are spent directly on diabetes research—the association calls it "the gift of hope." Featured items are Christmas cards with winning designs chosen in an ADA art contest, as well as other cards with contemporary, religious, or general sentiments. Calendars, ornaments, sugar-free candies, and other gift items are also included in the catalog.

MAKE A WISH. The Make-A-Wish Foundation is the largest wish-granting organization in the world. Their mission is to grant wishes for children between two-and-a-half and eighteen who are living with life-threatening illnesses. There are currently eighty-four chapters within the United States and fifteen international affiliates. Referrals come from parents, legal guardians, therapists, doctors, nurses, family members, and sometimes the children themselves. A team of wish "fairies" is sent to the child's home to help determine what the child's wish is. For more information about the Atlanta chapter, which serves greater Atlanta and northern Georgia, call 770-916-0082, or for more information about other chapters, contact the Make-A-Wish Foundation of America at 1-800-722-9474.

CONGRATS ON QUITTING! Call 1-800-LUNG-USA for a gift that congratulates someone who has given up smoking. Consider a donation to the American Lung Association, which has an "expressive gifts program" for those occasions when the best gift might be one that helps others. You decide how much you want to donate (there is no minimum), and the American Lung Association will send a card to the person you honor, notifying them of the gift without revealing the amount.

WITH UNICEF YOU GIVE HOPE. Call 1-800-FOR-KIDS and order UNICEF cards and gifts from the United States Committee for UNICEF, which provides clean water, health care, education, and nutrition programs for children and mothers in 137 underdeveloped countries. You'll find a variety of colorful and meaningful gifts in this catalog.

Presents for Other Special Days and Holidays

22

*E*ach year is filled with many fabulous occasions for giving presents. You don't have to wait until someone's birthday or anniversary—every day in its own right can be some kind of holiday. It's simply up to you to make it one. Perhaps you'll name a day in someone's honor, or remember the first time you met and call that cause for celebration.

The following suggestions fill in the gaps for the rest of those special days and holidays with fun ideas for each occasion. While I couldn't address every single holiday imaginable, keep in mind that many of the presents are interchangeable. Get creative and adapt an idea from another chapter. In the meantime, have a wonderful year filled with good times, good friends, and much health and happiness. Now go celebrate!

HOLIDAYS PLUS. Call 1-800-CELEBRATE and request the Celebration Fantastic catalog, which is filled with fabulous items for a wide variety of special days and holidays throughout the year. You'll find a unique selection of themed gifts perfect for every occasion, including artwork, accessories, books, bears, dolls, videos, goodies, clothing—all suitable for the appropriate season. This catalog is your one-stop shop for outstanding presents for special days.

LUCK OF THE IRISH. For St. Patrick's Day, consider giving the Claddagh door knocker, available in brass from the Irish Cottage at 1-800-338-2085. The Claddagh is an Irish symbol of lasting love and eternal friendship that shows two hands holding a heart. If you prefer something to be a little more whimsical, the shop also offers a leprechaun door knocker and a unique selection of presents with an Irish theme.

ST. PATRICK'S DAY. Celebrate the luck of the Irish with a greeting card attached to a box of Lucky Charms. If you want to give a special gift to someone special, you could hide it in the cereal. Bring on the milk—this gift promises to be lots of fun!

BRING ON THE GREEN. Package up a basket of green sweets, cookies, or snacks for an edible way to say "Happy St. Patrick's Day." From green pistachios to green mint candies, you'll find a surprising assortment of candy that's every imaginable shade of green at your local grocery store. Add a green ribbon and a note that says, "I might be a little green at this, but I think you're terrific. Happy St. Patrick's Day!"

SOME-BUNNY LOVES YOU! Celebrate Easter with a new twist and fill a basket with books about bunnies. Consider a copy of a book about a famous bunny, such as Peter Cottontail or Brer Rabbit. The card, of course, could say, "Have a hoppy Easter!"

PRESIDENTS' DAY. Okay, so you think no one gives gifts for Presidents' Day. But there are those of us who remember back when Washington's Birthday was a much bigger deal than it is today, and chocolate-covered cherries were a tradition. A box of chocolate-covered cherries would be great way to sweeten up the dead of winter, and it'd be an unexpected surprise. Add a card that reads, "I cannot tell a lie . . . I absolutely adore you!" or "Life's a bowl [box] of cherries thanks to you."

SECRETARIES' DAY. Give your assistant a real coffee break with a gift from J. Martinez & Co. at 1-800-642-5282. J. Martinez sells fine coffees from the company that introduced "estate" coffees to consumers. Available by the pound and half-pound in luxury packaging, these fine premium coffees are priced from $8.00 to $40.00 per pound. Also available are elegant and generously sized presentation gift boxes, which cost anywhere from $30.00 to $165.00. For a real awakening, order the chocolate-covered coffee beans. Gift or "presentation" packages can be made to your specifications.

FOR A SOUPER SECRETARY. If your secretary enjoys soups and snacks, why not give her a break and something to go with it? Fill a basket with a selection of instant soups that are easily made by adding hot water and include an assortment of snacks. Add a note that says, "For a souper secretary—we think you're the greatest!"

SPRING HAS SPRUNG. Easter and the coming of spring symbolize the renewal of life. Wildflower seeds are a great gift for anyone who enjoys flowers but doesn't have much of a green thumb. Just sprinkle the seeds on the ground and watch them grow and bloom. Since wildflowers have become popular, you can find seed packs in the gardening departments of most discount stores and home centers, as well as in most seed catalogs.

HOW CHIMING! To celebrate the first day of spring, give a set of wind chimes. Your card could read, "I just wanted to chime in and say hello."

LOOK WHAT'S COOKING. What's the Fourth of July without an Independence Day cookout? A timely gift would be a grilling gift pack, including grilling equipment (such as long-handled spatula and tongs), barbecue sauce, and flavorful grilling wood, such as mesquite or hickory chips.

SHOW YOUR COLORS. What better day than the Fourth of July to give someone a flagpole and flag? The Stars and Stripes are appropriate, of course, but if you visit a home or garden shop, you're likely to find a variety of colorful flags in themes from general summer items (such as a watermelon) to Americana (some version of red, white and blue). Include a short flagpole to be attached to the house. (And once you've given this gift, you've opened a whole new avenue of gift giving for yourself, because you can continue to give new seasonal and holiday-themed flags as the urge strikes you.)

ROSH HASHANAH. This religious holiday celebrates the Jewish New Year. A basket of apples and a jar of honey is the perfect gift to traditionally and symbolically usher in a sweet new year and will be appreciated to the core.

HALLOWEEN COVER-UP. For Halloween, give a kid a supply of theatrical makeup that's safe for the skin and easy to remove, so he can really look the part he's playing. It's also safer on Halloween not to cover up a child's vision with a mask that might give a limited range of vision. If you have any skills at applying makeup, offer to do the child's makeup or teach her how to do it herself.

GOBLIN UP A GOOD BOOK. Kids associate Halloween with candy, but you can give them food for the brain. How about a book of ghost stories? For younger kids, the *Goosebumps* series of books is popular. An older kid might actually enjoy a classic, such as a collection of Edgar Allen Poe stories.

A GIFT FOR ALL SEASONS. Call 1-800-776-9677 and order Seasons, a festive gift catalog that focuses on a wide variety of special occasions and holidays, including Valentine's Day, Halloween, Christmas, Hanukkah, and more. This outstanding resource has a wide selection of themed gifts, including accessories, clothing, jewelry, and books geared to family, friends, and holidays.

THANKSGIVING WITH HARRINGTON'S. Call 1-802-434-4444 and order a catalog from Vermont-based smoked meat house, Harrington's. Harrington's, which has been in business for over 125 years, specializes in mail-order meats. You'll find plenty of fully cooked main courses for your Thanksgiving feast or any holiday dinner for that matter. They also have a wide assortment of sauces, cheeses, breakfast delicacies, desserts, and more.

GIVING THANKS. Here's a company you'll be thankful you discovered. Call 1-903-595-0725 and order a delicious turkey from Greenberg Smoked Turkey for the perfect Thanksgiving gift. For sixty years, Greenberg has delivered turkeys to thousands of happy customers across the country. Consider a Greenberg turkey the perfect present, especially when you don't know what to send or bring to your next Thanksgiving celebration. And just in case you don't want to cook, your guests will think you're a kitchen wizard if you order one and serve it, too.

BAR/BAT MITZVAH GIFT. A Bar or Bat Mitzvah is a very special day symbolizing adulthood in the life of a Jewish thirteen-year-old, and it requires a great deal of studying and hard work. Consider a meaningful present that commemorates this event, like a mezuzah, a Star of David necklace, or their very own Hanukkah menorah. You'll find these and other wonderful presents at a local synagogue's gift shop. Or, call 1-800-426-2567 and order a catalog from the Source for Everything Jewish, which specializes in Judaica gifts.

MAZEL TOV! Say *mazel tov* to a smart cookie on their Bar or Bat Mitzvah! Call 1-800-BEST-GIFT (1-800-237-8443) and order a kosher cookie basket from the Clever Cookie Corporation that can be delivered anywhere. It will be personalized for the occasion with the recipient's name and a greeting, and anyone will love this edible gift filled with delicious cookies wrapped up in cellophane and a big bow. They also have a variety of cookie baskets for other holidays and special occasions, so keep their telephone number close by.

MAKE A MITZVAH. When giving a Bar or Bat Mitzvah boy or girl a check, add extra to your gift and request that they keep a portion and give the specified additional amount to a good cause in honor of their special day. For example, you could give $25.00, with $18.00 (the number that stands for *chai*, meaning "life") as your gift, and request that the additional $7.00 be donated to the cause of their choice.

If you or someone you know has given or received a perfect present, I'd love to hear from you for forthcoming books. Please send your name, address, telephone number, and suggestion to:

The Perfect Present
6300 Powers Ferry Rd., Suite 600-118
Atlanta, Georgia 30339

Product Sources

Adler & Company, 1-800-647-8007

American Association of Retired
  Persons (AARP), 1-800-424-3410

American Diabetes Association gifts,
  1-800-608-4279

American Girl's Collection,
  1-800-845-0005

*American Heart Association Cook-
  book, The,* 1-800-793-2665

*American Heart Association Kids'
  Cookbook, The,* 1-800-793-2665

American Lung Association
  (given-up-smoking gift),
  1-800-LUNG-USA

American Lung Association's
  Golf Privilege Card,
  1-800-LUNG-USA

Animazing Gallery, 1-800-303-4848

AT&T National Toll-Free Directory,
  1-800-426-8686

Austad's Golf, 1-800-759-4653

Back in the Saddle, 1-800-865-2478

Balducci's, 1-800-225-3822

Ballard Designs, 1-800-367-2775

Baseball Express, 1-800-WE-PITCH
  (1-800-937-4824)

Black Hound New York,
  1-800-344-4417

Blooming Cookies, 1-800-435-6877

Bloomingdale's by Mail, Ltd.,
  1-800-777-0000

Blue Heron Gift Fruit Shippers,
  1-800-237-3920

Borsheim's, 1-800-642-GIFT

British Links, 1-800-348-4646

Burpee Gardens, 1-800-283-5159

Byrd Cookie Company,
  1-800-291-BYRD

Cakes Across America,
  1-800-422-5387;
  www.cakesacrossamerica.com

Carnegie Delicatessen &
  Restaurants, 1-800-334-5606

Celebration Fantastic,
  1-800-CELEBRATE

Chef's, 1-800-338-3232

Chinaberry, 1-800-776-2242

Chocolate Emporium, 1-888-
  CHOCLAT; www.choclat.com

Christian Children's Fund Craft
  Cooperative, 1-800-366-5896

Clever Cookie Corporation, 1-800-
  BEST-GIFT (1-800-237-8443)

Colorful Images, 1-800-458-7999

Container Store, 1-800-733-3532

Country House, 1-800-331-3602

Craig 'n' Company, 1-800-552-4088

Crate & Barrel, 1-888-249-4155

Creole Foods of Opelousas,
  1-800-551-9066

Current, Inc., 1-800-643-0042

Cushman's, 1-800-776-7575

Danforth Pewterers, 1-800-222-3142

De Brito Chocolate Factory,
  1-800-588-3886

Della Robbia Wreath,
   1-800-833-7769
Dick Blick Art Materials,
   1-800-447-8192
Disney, 1-800-237-5751;
   www.disneystore.com
Doctors Foster and Smith,
   1-800-562-7169

Edwin Watts Golf Shops Pro-Line
   Golf Equipment, 1-800-874-0146
Eli's Cheesecake Company,
   1-800-ELI-CAKE (999-8330)
El Paso Chile Company,
   1-888-4-SALSAS
Elton candle, 1-888-44-ELTON
Elton's Angel, 1-800-CRISTAL
Erwin Pearl, 1-800-797-5378
Ethel M. Chocolates,
   1-800-4-EthelM

Fairytale Brownies,
   1-800-FAIRYTALE;
   www.brownies.com
Flying Noodle, 1-800-566-0599;
   www.flyingnoodle.com
Frontgate, 1-800-626-6488
Frontier Soups, 1-800-253-0550

Garden Botanika, 1-800-968-7842
Giftcorp, 1-800-440-2131;
   www.giftsbygiftcorp.com
Gifts of the Spirit, Daybreak Books,
   Rodale Press
*Gifts That Make a Difference: How to
   Buy Hundreds of Great Gifts Sold
   Through Nonprofits,* Foxglove Pub-
   lishing, P.O. Box 292500, Dayton,
   Ohio 45429-0500
Girl Scouts of America,
   1-800-221-6707

Godiva Chocolatier, 1-800-
   9-GODIVA; www.godiva.com;
   America Online: keyword Godiva
Great Catalog Guide, Consuumer
   Services Dept., Direct Marketing
   Association, 1111 19th St. NW,
   Ste. 1100, Washington, D.C.
   20036-3603
Great Kids Company,
   1-800-533-2166
Greenberg Smoked Turkey,
   1-903-595-0725

Hallmark at Home,
   1-800-983-4663
Hamaker Judaica, Inc.,
   1-800-426-2567
Hammacher Schlemmer,
   1-800-543-3366
Hammons Pantry, 1-800-872-6879
Happy Herman's, 1-800-825-6263
Harbor Freight Tools,
   1-800-423-2567
Harrington's, 1-802-434-4444
Harry and David, 1-800-547-3033
Hershey's Gift Catalog,
   1-800-4KISSES (454-7737)
Historic Newspaper Archives,
   1-800-221-3221

Illuminations, 1-800-CANDLES
Into the Wind, 1-800-541-0314
Irish Cottage, 1-800-338-2085

Jester Has Lost His Jingle, The
   (Saltzman), 1-800-9-JESTER
Jewish National Fund Tree
   Certificate Department,
   1-800-542-TREE (8733)
Jinil au Chocolat, 1-800-64-JINIL
J. Martinez & Co., 1-800-642-5282

Joe's Stone Crab, 1-800-780-CRAB (2722)

J. Peterman Company Catalog, 1-800-231-7341

Junior League Centennial Cookbook, The, Main Street Books, Doubleday

Kaplan Educational Centers, 1-800-KAP-ITEM

KiDoodles, 1-800-459-7215

Kosher Cornucopia, 1-800-7KOSHER; www.koshercornucopia.com

Kwanzaa: A Family Affair (Walter), Avon Books

Kwanzaa Fun: Great Things to Make and Do (Robertson and Pearson), Kingfisher

Legal Sea Foods, 1-800-343-5804

Levenger's, 1-800-544-0880

Levi Strauss & Co., 1-800-USA-LEVI

Life's Little Instruction Book (Brown), vols. 1 to 3, Rutledge Hill Press

Lilly's Kids, 1-800-285-5555

Little Things Shared: Lasting Connections Between Family and Friends (Newman), Crown Publishers

Livonia Collection, 1-800-543-8566

Lizell, 1-800-718-8808

L.L. Bean (fly-fishing catalog), 1-800-541-3541

L.L. Bean (sporting catalog), 1-800-221-4221

Made with Care, 1-800-521-CARE; www.care.org

Make-A-Wish Foundation of America, 1-800-722-9474

Mature Mart, 1-800-720-6278 (MART)

Mercedes-Benz, 1-800-FOR-MERCEDES

Ministry of Federal Star Registration, 1-800-528-STAR (8727) or 1-800-544-8814

Mori Luggage & Gifts, 1-800-678-MORI

mounting of journalism articles, 1-800-548-3993

Mozzarella Company, 1-800-798-2954

Mrs. Fields, 1-800-COOKIES; www.mrsfields.com

Mrs. London's Confections, 1-800-452-8162

Music Stand, 1-800-414-4010

My Twinn, 1-800-469-8946

Nordstrom, 1-800-285-5800

Omaha Steaks, 1-800-228-9055

Orvis Travel, 1-800-541-3541

Paragon, The, 1-800-343-3095

Personal Creations, 1-800-326-6626; 1-800-264-6626

Piece of Cake, 1-800-9-CAKE-90

Pooh Gram from Disney, 1-800-840-POOH

Pottery Barn, 1-800-922-5507

Present Perfect, 1-305-661-3032

Ralph Marlin & Co., Inc., 1-800-922-8437

Relax the Back, 1-800-290-2225

Road Runner Sports, 1-800-551-5558

Ross-Simons, 1-800-556-7376

San Francisco Music Box Company,
1-800-227-2190
Saxe 800 Birthstones, 1-800-BIRTH-
STONES
Sealed With A Kiss,
1-800-888-SWAK; www.swak.com
Seasons, 1-800-776-9677
Second Avenue Kosher Deli,
1-800-NYC-DELI
Send-A-Song, 1-800-SEND-A-
SONG
Sharper Image, 1-800-344-4444
Silver Queen, The, 1-800-262-3134
Simple Abundance (Breathnach),
Warner Books
Smith & Hawken, 1-800-776-3336
Softball Express, 1-800-WE-PITCH
(1-800-937-4824)
Songs-4-U, 1-800-447-3708
Source for Everything Jewish,
1-800-426-2567
Spiegel, 1-800-345-4500
Starbucks Coffee Company,
1-800-STARBUC (782-7282)
Steuben, 1-800-424-4240
Successories, 1-800-554-6257
Sugardale Foods, 1-800-860-4267
Sundance, 1-800-422-2770
Supergram, 1-800-3-BANNER
(322-6637)
Sur la Table, 1-800-243-0852
Suzanne's Mail Order Muffins,
1-800-742-2403
Thatcher's Special Popcorn,
1-800-926-CORN (2676)
Tiffany & Co., 1-800-526-0649
Tool Crib of the North,
1-800-358-3096

Treasured Collection,
1-800-729-2321

UNICEF cards and gifts,
1-800-FOR-KIDS
United States Postal Service,
1-800-STAMP-24
University of Texas M. D. Anderson
Cancer Center Children's Art Project, 1-800-231-1580

Vermont Teddy Bear Co.,
1-800-829-BEAR (2327)

Walter Drake, 1-800-525-9291
Warner Bros. Studio Stores,
1-800-223-6524;
www.studiostore.warnerbros.com
Western Union, 1-800-325-6000
What on Earth, 1-800-945-2552
*When Words Matter Most: Thoughtful
Deeds for Every Occasion* (New-
man), Crown Publishers
White Flower Farm, 1-800-503-9624
White House, Greetings Office,
Room 39, Washington, D.C.
20500
Wolf Camera, 1-800-643-WOLF
(9653)
Wolferman's Fine Breads,
1-800-999-0169
World Candy Store,
1-888-SNACK-U4EA
Wrinkled Egg, The,
1-800-736-3998

YAI General Store,
1-800-YAI-9914

About the Author

ROBYN FREEDMAN SPIZMAN is a consumer advocate with more than fifteen years' experience researching and reporting as "The Super Shopper" on NBC affiliate WXIA-TV. Well known nationally as "The Gift Guru," Robyn has also appeared on CNN, The Discovery Channel, and CNBC, and is a contributing writer for *Woman's Day*. Robyn is a teacher, lecturer, and author with numerous educational, parenting, and self-help publications to her credit. She lives in Atlanta, Georgia, with her husband and two children.

Notes